MARY
Mother *of the*
Redemption

MARY
Mother *of the*
Redemption

by E. Schillebeeckx, O.P.

Professor of Dogmatic Theology
and the History of Theology at
the Roman Catholic University of Nijmegen

translated by N. D. SMITH

SHEED AND WARD: New York

© *Sheed and Ward Ltd., 1964*

Originally published as *Maria,
Moeder van de verlossing*, Antwerp, Uitgeverij
Apostolaat van de Rozenkrans (1954) and
Bilthoven, Uitgeverij H. Nelissen (1963)

NIHIL OBSTAT:
JOANNES M. T. BARTON, S.T.D., L.S.S., CENSOR DEPUTATUS
IMPRIMATUR: ✠ PATRITIUS CASEY, VIC. GEN.

WESTMONASTERII, DIE 30 JUNII 1964

The Nihil obstat *and* Imprimatur *are a declaration that a
book or pamphlet is considered to be free from doctrinal
or normal error. It is not implied that those who have
granted the* Nihil obstat *and* Imprimatur *agree with the
contents, opinions or statements expressed.*

Library of Congress Catalog Card Number: 64-19913

Manufactured in the United States of America

NOTE

This translation is based on the third
revised Dutch edition, with further
revisions and additions by the author.

CONTENTS

ABBREVIATIONS

INTRODUCTION

IT IS IMPOSSIBLE to arrive at a sound interpretation of the Marian mystery in all its truly Christian depth in a treatise in which the subject is dissociated from the mystery of Christ. A true understanding can be achieved only when the mystery of Mary is allowed to develop fully within the mystery of Christ, as Mariology and Christology clearly do not exist as separate entities, but form a single organic whole. If this basic and self-evident view of the Faith is not accepted as the predominant guiding principle in our consideration of the Marian mystery, it is not entirely unreasonable to expect that the Christian redemption will, as a result, be seen in a false perspective, and that our treatment of the subject will detract from the fundamental tenet of Catholic dogma—namely, that we are redeemed by God. For we are indeed redeemed by God alone, but in and through the human form in which he manifested himself to us—we are redeemed through Jesus Christ, God become man. But, by virtue of our free consent, which is necessarily implied in the Redemption, all of us—and, in a very special and profound way, Mary—share, as human beings, in the Redemption. We are "co-redeemers," even though this takes the form of an "active receptiveness" towards the God-man, Christ, who is the only Redeemer.

This is one of the main reasons why the Church tends to avoid the Marian title of "co-redemptrix" in her official documents, and generally has recourse to less overcharged formulations, such as "partner in the Redemption." The Church is so profoundly aware of the fact that "Jesus" means "Yahweh has saved" that she feels that the term "co-redemption" might imply that Mary, though subordinate to Christ, was none the less complementary to him in the bringing about of the Redemption. The Church is absolutely convinced of the fact that there is one and only one Mediator between the Father and us, his children: "For there is one God; and one mediator of God and men, the man Christ Jesus, who gave himself a redemption for all, a testimony in due times." (1 Tim. 2. 5–6.) However unique Mary may be, and however all-embracing her role in the divine plan of salvation, the fact remains that all men, apart from Christ, the God-man and Redeemer, are essentially *redeemed* men. It would therefore be more accurate to speak of a personal communion with Christ who is *himself* the Redemption, for this implies a partnership in the Redemption.

On the other hand, the idea of Mary's exceptional place among redeemed humanity is the Church's sacred inheritance, common both to the Eastern and to the Western tradition. As the one who stands beside us in the long line of the redeemed, the Mother of God occupies a pre-eminent place. She is not simply one particularly important fellow member of the Mystical Body, but someone who is far more close and intimate—as the Mother of the whole Christ, the head of all the members of Christ's mystical body.

Two truths lie at the heart of the Marian mystery. Among redeemed mankind, the Mother of God is the most sublime human being of all and the firstfruit of the Redemption. At the same time, she is the mother of all redeemed mankind and, as such, her sway, within the redeemed world, is universal and extends to all those who are co-redeemed. In our examination of the subject we shall aim to reduce these two basic truths to one single vision, in order to bring out as clearly as possible the organic unity which exists between the various Marian mysteries and this single Mariological principle.

"Love gave her a thousand names."[1] But we know from experi-

[1] This is the first line of the popular Flemish hymn to Mary by Augustus

ence that love which is uninformed tends to express itself in exaggeration and to give a false interpretation of true greatness. As a vital part of the Church's life of faith and as a living organism acting within it, theology is both at the service of the Church's teaching office and under its control. It follows, then, that theology must act as the critical sounding-board of the Church's present preaching and, at the same time, prepare the way for her preaching in the future. This is why all theological study must attempt to penetrate more and more deeply into the unfathomable mystery of the reality of Mary within the plan of salvation, to help to dispense the inexhaustible riches of this reality and to divest it of everything which is not derived from revelation.

Theology has to be critical in its attitude towards the thousand names bestowed upon the Virgin Mother by popular devotion. But theology lives in and draws its sustenance from the life of faith led by the members of the Church community, and theologians should realize that this life is more powerful than all the feeble efforts made by theology. That is why theology, in exercising that criticism which is its rightful task, should never criticize in a spirit of self-satisfaction or theological "pride." It ought rather to recognize that the function of theological criticism is to serve the living, objective and absolute truth and humbly to acknowledge that every part of the truth possessed by any individual human being has a relative value. At the same time, theology must recognize too that it has freedom, when it is merely a question of discussing one or another proposition.

Although they had an ardent devotion to the Blessed Virgin, the great theologians of the Middle Ages were none the less extremely bold critics. They have warned us of the danger of bestowing false titles on Mary in an attempt to honour her, as she is already overendowed with glorious titles which are hers by right. As examples, we can quote the pseudo-Albert—"We do not aim to

---

Cuppens, "Onze Lieve Vrouw van Vlaanderen"—of all the thousand names which love has given to Mary, none is dearer to Flemish hearts than "Our Lady of Flanders."

adorn the glorious Virgin with our lies";[2] St. Bernard—"The honour of the Queen requires only truthfulness, the royal Virgin has no need of false honour, overendowed as she is with true titles of honour and adorned with the crown of many glories";[3] and St. Bonaventure—"We ought not to think up any new titles of honour in praise of the Virgin, who is well able to do without our lies, richly adorned as she is with the true glory."[4]

In his speech delivered on the eve of the Marian Congress in Rome in November 1954, Pope Pius XII also warned his listeners against the danger both of exaggeration in our attitude to Mary —in theological study, in the too energetic furtherance of devotions or from pure sentimentality—and of belittlement of the Marian mystery through extreme rationalization. In our examination of the subject we shall bear this salutary double warning constantly in mind. The best critical attitude towards this tendency to exaggerate either one way or the other is one which is positive, serene and objective, and which permits the author occasionally to stand aloof, on the one hand, from some of the excesses, and on the other, from an unchristian diminution of the true cult of Mary, in order to present a clearer argument.

[2] "Non intendimus gloriosam virginem nostris mendaciis adornare." (Pseudo-Albertus, *Mariale,* prooemium.)

[3] "Honor Reginae iudicium diligit, Virgo regia falso non egit honore, veris cumulata honorum titulis, infulis dignitatum." (St. Bernard, *Epist. CLXXIV,* 2 [*PL,* 182, col. 333].)

[4] "Non oportet novos honores confingere ad honorem Virginis, quae non indiget nostris mendaciis, quae tantum plena est veritate." (St. Bonaventure, *In III Sent.,* d. 3, pt. 1, a. 1, q. 2, ad 3.) See also Cajetan, *In Summam Theol.,* III, q. 7, a. 10, ad 1.

Mary,
Christ's Most Beautiful Creation:
God's Call to Us in Her

PART ONE

Mary,
Christ's Most Beautiful Creation;
God's Call to Us in Her

1

THE SCRIPTURAL IMAGE OF THE MOTHER OF JESUS

GOD'S ACTION IN HUMAN HISTORY

CHRISTIANITY IS NOT SIMPLY A DOCTRINE. First and foremost it is an *event*—the manifestation of a divine act in and through human history. Revelation is an existential event in which a divine reality impinges upon human realities in an earthly, visible form. It is thus a history of salvation—God *acting* in history and thereby coming to us in salvation. Our religion is concerned with the "Kingdom of God" which is *to come*. The Old Testament refers exclusively to the God who is to come, whereas the New Testament concentrates upon the advent of Christ and deals with his birth and the period he spends on earth with us, his departure, his sending of the Holy Ghost and his second coming. The Church is the Kingdom of God in a state of becoming.

Our history has been transformed into a *history of salvation* because God himself has entered it. Human history has thus become a highly significant succession of historical facts in which and through which God manifests himself as *our Redeemer*. God's act of redemption is both eternal and actually present at any given moment, and its manifestation in time, in events which take place in this world and in all the various acts performed by living human beings, has conferred a definitely historical dimension upon Redemption itself. Within this plan of salvation, *facts* are of the utmost importance—events, occurrences and men, both individually and communally, all play a decisive part in the course of the salvation of the whole of the human race. At the very heart of this history of man's salvation is the *man* Jesus, who is the living God himself, acting in a truly human, historical form. In Jesus history itself has become an episode in God's own personal life, and any single historical event is therefore transformed into a manifestation of the divine life of the Trinity, as a reality which vitally affects us human beings. A transhistorical dimension is thus conferred upon normal historical truth. From the purely historical point of view, Jesus is a man like other men—a man who becomes involved in human situations which lead to a conflict. The result of this conflict is that he appears, from the human point of view, to suffer defeat. In reality, however, the history of Jesus' life is a *theophany* —an act of God occurring within human acts which have been historically conditioned. It is a divine act which makes an immediate and direct attack upon us, seizing hold of us inwardly. It is, however, the history of this theophany within the divine plan of salvation which provides us with its concrete meaning and significance.

The Virgin from Nazareth is, after Christ, the principal person in this historical sequence of events. Mariology is therefore concerned with *the life of a person,* of one definite person in history. It is concerned with the mother of one definite person—Jesus of Nazareth. Mary is the mystery of a mother who had a child! Yet this historically conditioned life is the *revelation* of the divine act of redemption which became, in Mary's Child, a reality which was at the same time also a historical reality.

There are, then, two dimensions to the mystery of Mary. If we consider this mystery in its human and historical dimension, we obtain an insight into the quiet simplicity of a pious, homely woman of the people whose vision of life is steeped in the Old Testament and Jewish tradition, and who lives at a period in history when her country is under Roman occupation. Her life is, therefore, also influenced by the secular events arising from the contemporary political and religious situation in which the Jewish people find themselves. But, as this period of history is so meagrely documented, very many of the historical facts in Mary's life cannot be verified.

But the history of Mary's life is also a revelation. It is the tangible, visible and historical aspect of a suprahistorical dimension of the Marian mystery which affects the salvation of all men. It is for this reason that Scripture records only those human facts of Mary's life in which this suprahistorical dimension plays a decisive part. All the other human facts of the Virgin's life are of secondary importance compared with those human events which indeed have the special privilege of transmitting to us in a visible form God's suprahistorical act of redemption. These are the *kairoi* of Mary's life. All the other features are of secondary importance and simply make up the background to her life. Scripture tells us nothing about them, and if we wish to build up a reasonably accurate picture of this background, we can do this by research into the life and customs of the Palestine of that period rather than by scriptural research. The true significance of Mary can be understood only if we consider those of her human acts which played a *decisive* role in the Redemption. These form, in a very special way, the poles between which God's redemptive act breaks through into human history.

The ultimate aim of our analysis of this subject is to reveal the theological and suprahistorical significance of Mary's *kairoi*—of the historical but *decisive* human acts of Mary's life.

There is often something a little repellent about a study of a living person. We do not like to analyse someone with whom we have a loving relationship. All the same, God, Christ and Mary are entitled to receive the homage of our intelligence, so long as this is offered in the spirit of prayer.[1]

As what constitutes the basic structure of the Marian mystery, then, is a making visible of the divine intention to save mankind through the medium of human acts and events in this world, it is clear that we must first of all consider Mary as she appears in the plain, unadorned scriptural picture of her.

---

[1] In this context, see R. Guardini, *Die Mutter des Herrn,* Würzburg (1955).

THE LIFE OF FAITH
OF THE "HANDMAID OF THE LORD"

We are very often inclined to imagine that the life which Mary, Joseph and Jesus led together in the intimacy of their home in Nazareth was a kind of fairy-tale existence. How easy and how idyllically beautiful life must have been in a home filled with the sound of the divine Child's voice, in a home where every time the mother hugged her own child, she held divinity in her arms! But we may be sure that it was not like this at all. The living reality of the Holy Family was far from being that of a fairy-tale world. We tend to forget that the whole of Mary's earthly life was passed under the veil of a faith which neither saw nor comprehended, but continued to trust in the unfathomable dispensations of God's providence. We tend to forget the immense burden of Mary's life of faith, which has made her the "Queen of Confessors." We are prone to endow the Mary of history with a kind of intuitive vision of God in miniature, though this is never referred to either in Scripture or in tradition and is in fact contradicted in all genuine accounts, and especially in St. Luke's Gospel. Often we fail completely to grasp her true greatness: Mary's life of faith.

Mary spent the whole of her life in the severe ordeal of this faith—not comprehending, but believing, with a faith which increased through meditation and through living in close contact with the growing Child. St. Luke says this in so many words.[2] When the twelve-year-old Jesus was lost during the annual pilgrimage to Jerusalem, Scripture tells us that Mary and Joseph spent three sorrowful days in search of him. Then, when his mother, finding him in the Temple, reproached him for having caused his parents

[2] We do not know whether St. Luke was personally acquainted with Mary or not. His most important source of information must in any case have been St. John, in whose house Mary lived after Jesus' death. Furthermore, it is extremely likely that St. Luke also made use of Hebrew and Aramaic documents. This is borne out, for example, by the fact that the part of his gospel dealing with Christ's early life contained several metrical hymns, that there are many obviously Semitic usages in this account—in striking contrast to the rest of the gospel—and finally that St. Luke himself makes vague allusions to such documents in the prologue to his gospel.

so much grief, he replied: "Did you not know that I must be about my Father's business?" To this, St. Luke adds that Joseph and Mary did not understand what Christ said. (2. 50.) This inspired text is of the greatest importance for us. In the Middle Ages it was popularly believed that Mary had a vision of the whole of Christ's life in all its phases at the moment of the Annunciation. This is, however, a false view, which deprives Mary of her greatness and of her great suffering, both of which are derived from the darkness of a faith which surrenders unconditionally to an uncomprehended mystery and an unknown future. Mary's life of faith on this earth is much closer to our own than the pretty pious legends that have gathered around the Holy Family. If we realize this, Mary's example will have a very much more powerful impact upon our own lives—she experienced the same difficulties in life as we do in ours, but always she submitted, in faith and in prayerful meditation, to the incomprehensible events of her life of which God was the Author.

Mary knew from the angel's message that her Jesus was to be the Redeemer, the royal Messiah who would redeem her people. That her Child was, however, truly God—God made man—is a truth which even Christ was to allow to filter through very carefully and slowly, drop by drop, into the minds of the Apostles. The *full* truth of Christ's divinity dawned upon them only with the Resurrection. The human—and even more particularly, the Jewish —mind had to be prepared gradually to receive such an enormous truth.

THE CONTENT AND MEANING
OF THE ANGEL'S MESSAGE

With particular reference to what Christ is to be, the message is as follows:

(1) "Rejoice,[3] full of grace, the Lord is with thee; blessed art

[3] S. Lyonnet has provided convincing proof that *chaire* does not mean "Hail!" in St. Luke, but "Rejoice!" (*laetare*). What we have here is that note of joy which characterizes every messianic annunciation; it is therefore not a mere greeting (*ave*). See *BA*, 20 (1939), pp. 131–41. For the following analogies, see also R. Laurentin, *Court traité de théologie mariale* (Paris, n.d.).

thou among women." (Luke 1. 28.) Mary at once senses that a messianic message is contained in this speech. She is bewildered by it. The angel, following the normal pattern of Semitic parallelism, then takes up again his first theme:

v. 28: Rejoice, full of grace,[4] the Lord is with thee.[5]	*v.* 30: Fear not, for thou hast found grace with God, *v.* 31: thou shalt conceive in thy womb.

(2) In the second parallel verse the vague "the Lord is with thee" is more clearly formulated: "Thou shalt bring forth a son."

This text clearly has very close affinities with Zephaniah [3. 14–17]:

ZEPHANIAH	LUKE
Rejoice,	Rejoice,
O daughter of Jerusalem,	full of grace,
Yahweh, the King of Israel, is in the midst of thee,	the Lord is with thee;
Fear not,	Fear not,
Sion,	Mary,
Yahweh, thy God, is in the midst of thee,[6]	thou shalt conceive in thy womb and shalt bring forth a son,
he is mighty; he will save	and thou shalt call his name

---

[4] It is advisable not to regard this as an adjective, but rather as the participle of a verb, as in Greek: *kecharitomene* ("receiving *charis*").

[5] The "Lord," Adonai, is Yahweh.

[6] "In thy midst"—in exceptional cases [Gen. 25. 22], this can mean the same as "in thy womb."

| [*yoshia*] | Jesus [*yoshua*: "Yahweh, the Saviour," "Yahweh has saved"] |

We shall return later to this parallelism and examine its implications more closely.

(3) The third part of the angel's message indicates that the Messiah is of the lineage of David. It is possible to discover numerous references in this part to the Old Testament, but the most striking parallel is with 2 Sam. 7. 12–16, in which the prophet Nathan addresses David:[7]

LUKE	SAMUEL
v. 32: He shall be *great*	*v.* 12: I will *raise up* thy seed after thee [=thy lineage], which shall proceed out of thy bowels; and I will establish his kingdom.
and shall be called the Son of the Most High.	I will be to him a father: and he shall be to me a son.
And the Lord God shall give unto him	*v.* 16: And thy house shall be faithful, and thy kingdom for ever before thy face:
the throne of David his father;	and thy throne shall be firm for ever.
And of his kingdom there shall be no end.	*v.* 13: And I will establish the throne of his kingdom for ever.

(4) Finally, the Child's transcendent origin is mentioned: "The Holy *Ruah* [Ghost] shall come upon thee and the power of the

---

[7] We are taking fully into account here the Greek Septuagint, which St. Luke knew and used (with the result that his version displays closer affinities with the Septuagint—this, however, raises very few difficulties).

Most High shall overshadow thee. And therefore that which shall be born of thee shall be called holy, the Son of God."[8]

It is not possible to find any passage in the Old Testament which is directly parallel to this one. We should note, however, that this message is closely connected with the Old Testament idea of *shekinah,* or God's presence on earth, which is often accompanied by the overshadowing of a cloud. A cloud covered the Ark of the Covenant [see Exod. 40.32–36] and there is also mention of a cloud in connection with the Transfiguration and the Ascension. What we have here, then, is the presence of Yahweh.

In addition we might consider the text which is complementary to that of the angelic salutation—the verses which are concerned with the Visitation:

(5) Elizabeth praises Mary with the words "Blessed art thou that hast believed" (Luke 1. 45) and glorifies her (Luke 1. 42) The parallel here is with Judith 13. 23–4:

JUDITH	LUKE
Blessed art thou, O daughter, by the Lord, the most high God, above all women upon the earth.	Blessed art thou among women
Blessed be the Lord who made heaven and earth.	and blessed is the fruit of thy womb.

(6) The Magnificat echoes the Old Testament in every one of of its separate parts. This becomes especially clear if the Greek version of the Magnificat is compared with the Septuagint.[9]

LUKE (1. 46–55)	SEPTUAGINT
My soul magnifies the Lord,	My heart leaps up in the Lord,

---

[8] There have been very many different translations of this passage. The problem presented by the meaning of "the Son of God" is also of some importance. In addition to the translation given above, the following is also plausible: "therefore also the Holy which shall be born of thee shall be called the Son of God." (Douai.)

[9] This is assuming that St. Luke sees Mary as Israel personified.

and my spirit cries out with joy in God, my Saviour.

my strength is exalted in God and rejoices in thy salvation. [Canticle of Hannah,[10] 1 Sam. 2. 1.]

Because he looks down upon the poverty [lowliness, humility] of his handmaid.

Deign to look down upon the poverty [humility] of thy handmaid. [I Sam. I. II.]

Behold, from henceforth, all generations shall call me blessed.

I am blessed, for all women call me happy. [Gen. 30 13.]

For he that is mighty has done great things to me, and holy is his name.

He is thy God who has done mighty things for thee. [Deut. 10.21.] Holy is his name. [This phrase occurs very frequently in the Old Testament.]

His mercy is from generation to generation upon them that fear him.

The mercy of the Lord is from eternity to eternity; his mercy is upon them that fear him. [Ps. 102 (103). 17.]

He shows the strength of his arm and scatters the proud.

There are many parallels to these verses in the Old Testament: Ps. 88 [89]. 13; 2 Sam. 22. 28; 1 Sam. 2. 4–7; Ps. 146.6; 32[33]. 10; 106[107]. 9; Job 12. 19 etc.

He puts down the mighty from their throne, but exalts the lowly.

He fills the hungry with gifts and the rich he sends empty away.

[10] This very close parallel also expresses joy over the miraculous birth of a child (Samuel), which God gave to Hannah, who was barren. The overtones of this and other closely related cases in the Old Testament must obviously have been very clear to pious Jews who were brought up on the Bible.

He has taken pity[11] on Israel, his servant, being mindful of his mercy.	Thou, Israel, my servant, on whom I have taken pity. Isa. 41.8; see also Ps. 97 (98).3.]
As he spoke to our fathers, to Abraham and his seed for ever.	As thou hast sworn to our fathers from the days of old [Mic. 7.20], to David and his generation for ever [2 Sam. 22. 51; Gen. 17. 7; 18. 18; 22. 17–18].

It is far from the author's intention to claim that precisely those particular texts, detailed in the above list, are revived in the Magnificat. This claim can certainly be made in the case of the Canticle of Hannah and the other texts which refer to miraculous birth, but for the rest the parallels only go to show that the Magnificat is a typical expression of the biblical religiosity of Israel. What we have here is a Jewish woman who believed in the Word of God, whose life was founded on Old Testament spirituality and who drew her sustenance from the Bible. Consequently, when she prayed to God or spoke about him, she did so in biblical texts which she had committed more or less accurately to memory. Christ himself did the same when he was on the Cross, and we also do so in our frequent use of the Psalms in the Liturgy. In this way, we are able to understand how, when she heard the angel's message, various biblical texts spontaneously came into Mary's mind.

If we analyse all these texts very carefully, the conclusion which we are bound to come to is, on the one hand, that they are in complete accord with the Old Testament ideas concerning the Messiah, and on the other, that they undoubtedly contain certain clear indications that the angelic message did convey to Mary some inkling that her Child really was God. Let us consider this in greater detail.

[11] Both Luke and Isaiah use the verb *antilambanomai* ("to have pity on, be sorry for, someone"). The phrases which follow—"as he spoke" and "as thou hast sworn"—are both closely connected with the idea of "mercy" referred to in the preceding verse by Luke, and by Micah.

The "Son of the Most High" and the "Son of God"

In the Jewish religion this title was used in a very general sense, but in many instances it was also applied concretely.[12] The Jewish race was called the "Son of God." (Exod. 4. 22; Deut. 1. 31.) Every just man calls himself the "son of God." (Wis. 2. 13, 16.) Whoever keeps the Law is the "son of the Lord." The Jews, who are members of the Chosen Race, will be called the "sons of the living God." (Hos. 1. 10.) Princes and judges especially are the "sons of the Most High" (Ps. 81. 6), and the kings of Israel, the Lord's anointed, are also called Yahweh's "sons" (2 Sam. 7. 14; 1 Chron. 17. 13 etc.). The royal Messiah is, moreover, heralded in the Psalms as the "son of God." (Ps. 2 and 88.) And when Christ is called the "Son of God" in the Synoptic Gospels, it is generally in this same moral and generally religious sense. (E.g., Matt. 4. 3; Mark 3. 12; Luke 4. 41 etc.) It is of course true that

---

[12] See especially P. Benoit, O.P., "La Divinité de Jésus dans les évangiles synoptiques," in *LV* (1953), no. 9 (pp. 43–74, especially 54–63). Benoit begins his examination of the New Testament idea of the *filius Dei* thus: "It would at first sight appear that the first of these titles ('Son of God— Son of Man') is the strongest and the clearest and that this should be sufficient to settle the question once and for all. If Jesus really did refer to himself as the Son of God, if he agreed to let others call him by this title, the question is clear: since the Synoptic Gospels, Christ's divinity has been established—no further discussion of the subject is necessary. But the matter is not, in fact, quite so simple as that, since this title has not always had the exact and transcendent meaning which, thanks to the New Testament texts, the Christian religion has bestowed upon it, and which it has acquired as a result of theological speculation and the consequent formulation of dogmas on the subject. What it means for us is the ontological sonship of a being who possesses a divine nature by reason of the fact that he was eternally begotten in the bosom of the Father. But before reaching the stage where this specific definition was made, the formula had a long history, in the course of which the type of sonship which it denoted was much more loosely defined, and of a moral, not of a metaphysical nature." (Pp. 54–5.) Benoit goes on to say that the title "Son of Man," which Jesus prefers to use of himself, places greater emphasis on his divinity than that of "Son of God." In this context, see also J. Dupont, "Filius meus es tu, L'interprétation du Psaume 2. 7 dans le Nouveau Testament," in *RSR* (1948), no. 35, pp. 522–43.

at the period when the Evangelists were actually writing the Gospels, they had, mainly because of their experience of the Resurrection (the supreme revelation of Christ's divinity), an explicit belief in the divinity of Christ, with the result that the phrase "the son of God" tended to convey a much more profound and dogmatic meaning to those who heard it.[13] But what we are dealing with here is the situation in which those who heard this phrase *before* Jesus' full revelation found themselves in fact. This is especially important to bear in mind in the case of the Annunciation. All we know from this is actually what Mary herself knew for certain at that time about her Child. If the words of the Message are considered on their own, all that Mary could have understood from them was that her Son was to be the long-awaited Messiah, the Great One who, being sent from God, was thus very intimately connected with God.[14]

It is precisely because of this intimate connection with God, which is apparent in the special intervention of God's spiritual power which is to overshadow Mary, that the Child is called the "Son of God."[15] The phrase "Son of God" was readily available, as

[13] It is probable that this gradually developed belief in Christ's divinity, based upon the fact of the Resurrection and even more particularly upon the subsequent miracle of Pentecost, exerted a retroactive influence upon the Evangelists in their account of Christ's acts, sayings and sermons prior to Easter and Pentecost. Much of what Christ may have expressed with deliberate vagueness may, because of this, have been heightened in the Evangelists' reports, and again, the meaning of some of his statements may not have been fully understood by the Apostles until after the Resurrection. Exegetes have pointed to many examples in the Synoptic Gospels of such retroactive influences.

[14] As early as 1921, Lagrange wrote: "It is better to recognise that the text does not provide the entire doctrine of the Incarnation, rather than to force it to give the meaning we are looking for." (*L'Évangile selon S. Luc,* Paris [1921], p. 36.) Elizabeth's commendation of Mary's faith has clearly to do with her belief in the Virgin Birth: "Blessed is she who believed that what was said to her by God would truly be accomplished." (Luke 1.45, Greek text.) It should be noted that the above is a *purely exegetical* view.

[15] The word "therefore" must be taken to refer to God's overshadowing rather than to Mary's virginity—in this way, Christ's true divinity can be seen to be partially revealed in this text. If, on the other hand, "therefore"

the term currently used for the Messiah to whom the royal throne of David would be given—this is in fact also explicit in the text of the Annunciation. What the angel actually says is, "Jesus, the royal Messiah, shall be born from thy virgin womb." If the *explicit* words of the Message are considered *on their own,* then it must be concluded that no clear or precise statement is made concerning the divinity of Christ.

Mary's Consciousness of Jesus' Divinity

It goes, however, without saying that, in addition to having the contents of the Message conveyed to Mary, God also inwardly enlightened her spirit. In considering the religious depth of Mary's complete submission in faith to the incalculable mystery which was presented to her, we should not fail to take into account the true supernatural essence of faith—the "light of faith" by which God's spirit penetrates into the human spirit and seizes hold of it in order to focus its regard on what has been definitely revealed. If we do this, we are bound to conclude that, though it is not yet explicit, everything is in a very real sense already present in Mary's *fiat* which will later grow, in her life and through her constant contact with her divine Son, to a state of explicit clarity. At the same time, however, it is necessary for us also to see the essential relation of the operation of God's spirit—the "light of faith"—not only to the explicit nature of the words of the Message, but also to the

---

were taken to refer specifically to Mary's virginity, this could not be so, because this virginity could not be the reason for Mary's Son to be truly God. For a further developed belief in the Trinity, the direct intervention of the "spirit and power of God" (which must be interpreted, in the light of fuller understanding of the Faith, as the Holy Ghost) may certainly constitute the reason why the Word, also in his humanity, was in fact the true Son of the Father. The fact that many different translations have been suggested for this text is in fact also due to the dogmatic, positive meaning which is applied to the phrase "Son of God": e.g., "The Holy One that is to be born of thee shall be called the Son of God," "What shall be born shall be holy, and shall be called the Son of God," "What shall be born shall be called holy, the Son of God."

implicit trends of Old Testament messianism which culminate in the Message.

Even though the divinity of the Messiah was not recognized in the Old Testament—that is to say, not explicitly acknowledged—there is, nonetheless, a marked tendency in this direction in many Old Testament texts, highly significant for a believer.

In the first place the royal Messiah, the Great One sent from God, was undoubtedly thought of as being very intimately connected with God. The royal Messiah was a powerful reality for the Jews—so powerful, in fact, that it was for them almost as if this Messiah and Yahweh were identical.[16]

Secondly, there is the Old Testament messianic idea of the "son of man," and this certainly led to the development of a concept of a transcendent Messiah. The foundations of this concept were laid by Ezechiel, and a definite form was given to it by Daniel (7. 13).[17] The "son of man" would be a "heavenly" man, coming with the clouds of heaven. This means that two concepts developed alongside each other—that of the Messiah of David's lineage, who was always thought of purely as a man, and that of the Messiah of heavenly descent.

Finally—and this is probably the most important of these tendencies—the Old Testament does to some extent disclose a double vision of the Redemption. Yahweh himself is the Redeemer, leading his chosen but repeatedly unfaithful people towards salvation, and intervening constantly on this people's behalf. This activity on Yahweh's part gave rise to the conviction that he would *himself* take definite action "at the end of time." The prophet is referring to the coming of Yahweh as Redeemer when he says: "Prepare ye the way of the Lord, make straight in the wilderness the paths of

[16] See, for example, J. de Fraine, S.J., "De oud-oosterse Koningsidee in't Oude Testament," in *BA*, 14 (1953), pp. 117–30, and especially pp. 127–30; the theme is especially prominent in Scandinavian Protestant theology, e.g., H. Ringgren, "König und Messias," in *ZAW*, 64 (1952), pp. 120–47.

[17] See A. Feuillet, "Le Fils de l'homme de Daniel et la tradition biblique," in *RB*, 60 (1953), pp. 170–202, 321–46; cf. J. L. Leuba, *L'Institution et l'événement*, Neuchâtel and Paris (1950), esp. pp. 9–17. (Bibl. Théol. protestante.)

our God." (Isa. 40. 3.) It is Yahweh himself who will create a new heaven and a new earth (65. 17) and it is he who will rule over all nations (2. 3). Viewed from this standpoint, the history of Israel is a history of the *gesta Dei*—a history of divine intervention, resulting in decisive judgement on the part of Yahweh, who will ultimately "live" forever in the world. Yahweh is thus the redeeming God.

But, in addition to this vertical eschatological line running through the Old Testament, it is also possible to detect, as it were, a corresponding horizontal line of eschatological thought, which is not directly concerned with Yahweh, but with the one who is to come, the awaited Messiah. This Messiah is a *person*—a man who is to be the instrument with which Yahweh will put his plan of salvation into operation at the end of time. The transcendent eschatological idea and the messianic vision of the Old Testament gradually draw more closely towards each other, until they are eventually synthesized in God the Redeemer made man. Jesus is at the same time the God who is to come and the man who is to come.

In the message of the angel Mary is the exponent of the Old Testament expectation of God and the Messiah. She is the synthesis and the ultimate expression of Israel's messianic desire. This is St. Luke's conception of Mary in the Magnificat. She is presented in this light in the writings of the Church Fathers, and contemporary theologians have returned to this view. The grace of her immaculate conception and her total dedication to God in virginity made her especially sensitive and receptive to the action and effects of the light of faith. For this reason she provided, in her own person, the basic requirement of open receptiveness towards the lines of Old Testament expectations of "Yahweh the Redeemer" which in the Old Testament were already focusing on one single point.

We can best arrive at an understanding of what occurred inwardly in Mary's spirit by approaching the question from outside, as it were, through a comparison of the relevant Old Testament texts with what is explicitly stated in the Message, as handed down to us by St. Luke.

If the scriptural parallelism is taken fully into account (see the parallel texts given above), it can be seen that Mary is regarded, in the first part of the Message, as the personal summing-up of Israel.[18] The Yahweh who comes as a Saviour "in the midst of" or even "inside" Israel (Zephaniah) is, as we have already seen, parallel to Jesus, that is, Yahweh the Saviour, whom Mary conceives in her womb (Luke). Mary, living in the stream of Old Testament messianism, had a presentiment of the profundity of this tremendous reality, the Son of God. In a confused but nonetheless very real way, she was conscious of the deeper implication of her motherhood—that God himself, who had once come into Israel's womb, was now to enter her womb. Furthermore, the allusion to the *shekinah,* or overshadowing, served to confirm the presence of God. In the parallelism which exists between Judith and Luke there is also a mystical, or veiled reference—the "blessed fruit of her womb" calls to mind the "Lord who made heaven and earth." The same idea is present, too, in the interior parallelism within St. Luke (1. 28. 31)—"the Lord [i.e., God] is with thee" and "thou shalt conceive a son"—the latter being a more precise formulation of the former.

It is important, too, to note that Mary had an immediate presentiment that something quite unique was about to take place as soon as the angel began to speak. Her initial reaction to the angel was quite different from that of Zachariah, who was thrown into consternation by the angel's *appearance*: "Zachariah, seeing him, was troubled and fear fell upon him." (Luke 1. 11–12.) In marked contrast, Mary, the lowly one, was troubled by the first *words* which the angel addressed to her, and wondered what they could mean. (Luke 1. 29.) She experienced this reaction because her modesty made it difficult for her to realize that this profound mystery was intended for her.

[18] For a closer examination of the question of Mary and Israel, see A. M. Dubarle, "Les Fondements bibliques du titre marial de Nouvelle Ève," in *RSR,* 39 (1951), pp. 49–64; A. G. Hébert, "La Vierge Marie, Fille de Sion," in *VS,* 85 (1951), pp. 127–40.

If we place Mary in this way at the summit of all the Old Testament expectations of God and then picture her in conversation
with the angel of the Annunciation, it is not difficult to understand
how the whole of the Old Testament reality burst into life in her
soul, seized as it was by God's spirit. Attentive to the Message,
Mary is the exponent of the expectations of all Israel and she
realizes too that this Child which she, though a virgin, is to bear
as a virgin, is not simply an ordinary human child with an exceptional religious mission, but at the same time a Child whose nature
far exceeds all human comprehension.

Mary's religious life did not, therefore, develop from a state
of "positive not-knowing" or ignorance towards a state of positive
recognition and knowledge, but rather from an implicit but real
awareness to an explicit consciousness. Put in another way, her
life of faith is marked by a transition from awareness to knowledge, just as, in the life of the Church, even after revelation had
been brought to a close, an intuition of faith precedes the dogmatic definition which naturally is its ultimate outcome.

One can express this thought in another way, by applying the
words of St. Thomas Aquinas to Mary's situation: *"Mary's* act
of faith does not ultimately bear upon an explicit formulation *of
the Annunciation,* but it does express the reality *of the Word made
flesh."*[19] The inward appeal and the interior illumination of the
"light of faith" provides the intimate contact between Mary's personal act of faith and the objective reality of the virgin birth of
the Son of God. If this had not been present from the very outset,
then it would certainly not be possible to refer to the growth of
Mary's faith—developing as a result of her ever-increasing intimacy
with the reality of the incarnate God who was growing to manhood in her own home—as an inward growth stemming from an
initial acceptance of faith. It this were so, it would not be an interior development, but rather an outward appendage.

This interior growth of Mary's faith within the intimation which

[19] Cf. II–II, q. 1, art. 2, ad 2. The italics indicate where we adapt St.
Thomas's text.

she had of her Son's nature is clearly indicated in Scripture: she did not understand what Christ said (Luke 2. 50), "his father and mother were wondering at those things which were spoken concerning him" (2. 33), and they were astonished by what they saw in the Temple (2. 48). Moreover, it is important to remember that the Message did not imply that revelation had been brought to a close, even as far as Mary was concerned. It was, on the contrary, accomplished, for her too, in and through the gradual unfolding, in history, of Jesus' life.

Our object here is certainly not to deal with the purely psychological question as to whether knowledge is in the last resort a subtly varied reality, capable of including many different shades of psychological emphasis. We are concerned with the growth of faith in the religious life of the individual, and a supreme example of this is provided by Mary. It is clear that St. Luke had a definite purpose in mind when he included all the texts quoted above in his gospel. But they would become quite meaningless were we to deny that Mary's religious life was a growth towards explicit faith. On the assumption, then, that her religious life is marked by this growth, it is quite obvious that a whole phase of development took place in Mary's life of faith between the Annunciation and Christ's first public appearance during the wedding feast at Cana. This development was the result of her intimate, day-to-day association with her Child during the hidden years of his life. These years were hidden from men, but for Mary they were a gradual revelation of the mystery of Christ. The Message gave Mary no direct information about the future suffering of the Redeemer, and she would have had no foreknowledge of this, unless she herself recalled, at the time of the Message, the prophetic visions of the "suffering servant" figure spoken of in the Old Testament. When Jesus was forty days old, however, his stature and her own appeared in a totally new perspective. This new element was announced by Simeon, when he told Mary: "Behold, this child is set for the fall and for the resurrection of many in Israel and for a sign which shall be contradicted. And thy own soul a sword shall pierce." (Luke 2. 34–5.) Yet, although Christ's sacrificial death is undoubtedly the climax of the entire mystery of Christ, no reference is made to it in the Message! The Gospel does, however, record that events occurred, when Christ was twelve years old, which were still incomprehensible to Mary. (Luke 2. 50.)

Since Mary disappeared from the scene, so to speak, from the time of the miracle at Cana until the Crucifixion,[20] and thus did not follow the course of Christ's preaching and miracles as the Apostles did, it is evident that Jesus' hidden life, spent in close intimacy with his mother, played an active part in his revelation as far as she was concerned. The Apostles got to know Jesus through his preaching. Mary, on the other hand, got to know him more through his actions. But, in the intimacy of their life together in Nazareth, Jesus and his mother must have talked and listened to each other a great deal. Their conversations were certainly not on the fairy-tale level, and we can be sure, too, that they did not talk about miracles, nor did they even discuss in advance the Crucifixion and Resurrection. No, their conversations undoubtedly took the form of an interchange on the deepest religious level—a religious give-and-take. But, however curious we may be, we shall never learn the substance of this interchange, for Mary's modesty has concealed it from us. It must remain the secret of her own intimate religious life. One thing, however, must have struck her with particular force—the messiah's obedience to a human person, his mother. This we can know for certain, for she confided the fact, probably via St. John, to St. Luke, and the Evangelist recorded it factually, but with loving admiration, in that part of his gospel which deals with Christ's early life.

Our task here is to consider the depth of Mary's religious life and its growth towards explicit faith in and through her intimacy and daily contact with Christ's humanity. We are also particularly concerned with the fact that, by reason of this growing faith, Mary is a pre-eminent example for us. The great privilege which she enjoyed, as the immaculate Mother of Christ, does not make her an exception to the basic law to which every Christian on earth

[20] It is as if she concluded, from what Jesus said to her at Cana, "My hour is not yet come," that her hour too had not yet come.

is subject—the gradually maturing spiritual life of *faith,* which does *not* thrive on a constant succession of external visions; it should not be forgotten that only *one vision* was granted to Mary. On the contrary, according to this fundamental law, applicable to Mary and to every Christian, faith is nourished by contact, in belief, hope and love, with the living reality of salvation. For us this reality is God himself, who gives his living humanity to us in the sacraments of the Church. For Mary it was the God who was given to her as her own Child, the holy Person whom she called Jesus. In this sense, therefore, Mary is the prototype of the Church in pilgrimage on earth, just as she is also, as the *Assumpta,* the prototype of the permanent Church, established in heaven.

What St. Luke recorded in his account of Jesus' hidden life— "And his mother kept all these words in her heart" (Luke 2. 51) —undoubtedly synthesizes the whole of Mary's attitude towards the mystery of Christ as it unfolded itself before her eyes. When exactly did the powerful knowledge of this faith break through in all its clarity and illuminate her whole life? Was it before the miracle of Cana? Or was it earlier than this, or perhaps later, as in the case of the Apostles? Did she know, with a clear and unclouded knowledge, as we know now, when she was standing at the foot of the Cross? Or was this precisely her great agony, her share in the suffering of her Son at the Crucifixion, that her faith in the mystery of a "crucified Messiah" who was to die, though indestructible, was still obscure? For us, this must remain a mystery. If it were so, her experience of the grace of Pentecost must have been most profound. But there is no question here of any definite period of time. What is of the utmost importance is that spiritual reality, proceeding from her complete submission, in faith, to the total concrete mystery of Christ and from her gradually maturing intuition, which, though not explicit, was already present in a positive form from the very beginning and eventually broke through with startling clarity.

In any case, I feel that it would be fundamentally wrong to place

more emphasis on the explicit nature and complete foreknowledge of Mary's faith than on the far greater religious merit of a
self-sacrificing faith which does not calculate in advance, but rather
allows credit for unmeasured quantities and as yet unknown future
events which would seem to contradict the idea of the "royal" Messiah contained in the angel's message. It is quite clear that Mary's
faith was always coming up against contradictions. The Prophets
foretold that the Messiah would be a king and that the govern-
ment would be upon his shoulders, yet he was born to Mary in a
cave, because—as St. Luke observes—there was no room "for
them"—that is, for a man and a pregnant woman—in the public
caravanserai. What is more, she was obliged to seek refuge in
Egypt with that Child whose future was to mean so much for
Israel. The same "royal" Child grew up later in quite ordinary
human circumstances which attracted the attention of nobody.
The final contradiction for Mary must have been to see her King
go to an inglorious death on the Cross. Mary had no idea how
everything would eventually turn out, but she continued to believe and to trust in the Message, hoping against hope. She did
not experience that weakness to which the Apostles' faith was
prone, but the events of Christ's life must have been for her, as
they were for the Apostles, a staggering and silent mystery. Is it
not possible to see in Abraham's sacrifice a type of Mary's attitude
towards her Son? Like Abraham, Mary went with her only Child
to offer him to God. Abraham, believing in hope against hope
(Rom. 4. 18), was ready to sacrifice his son, although Israel's
great inheritance had been promised to this son, through his de-
scendants. Mary also offered her Son, to whom, according to the
Message, an incorruptible kingdom had been promised, yet she
saw him die on the Cross. Christ's death on the Cross was Mary's
sacrifice of Abraham, and she persisted in her faith in God, despite
all the outward signs which seemed to contradict it.

Thus Mary, believing utterly in the fact that her Child was the
royal Messiah and the Son of God, gradually came to the full
conception of what this mystery contained for her and for all

human kind. Even during his public life Jesus still had to reveal personally to his mother that he, though he remained her own Son, was ultimately quite independent of her. Even when he was only twelve years old, he had astonished his mother, during the pilgrimage to Jerusalem, by his self-confidence and independence. He showed the same independence during the marriage at Cana.[21] No reproach is implied in the words he addressed to Mary, as the earlier Church Fathers asserted—they constitute one more aspect of the total mystery of Christ which was being gradually revealed to Mary in the most intimate manner. This is also true of the few recorded events in Christ's public life in which Mary plays a part. A typical example of this is Christ's correction of the enthusiastic remark made by the woman in the crowd—"Blessed is the womb that bore thee!" (Luke 11. 27)—and of the information that was brought to him by various people to the effect that his mother was outside, looking for him (Matt. 12. 46–50; Mark 3. 31–5; Luke 8. 19–21). Jesus has no intention here of disparaging Mary, nor does he underestimate her true greatness—on the contrary, for he says, "Yea, rather, blessed are they who hear the word of God and keep it." (Luke 11. 27–8.) This is surely the highest praise of our Lady's religious life—the best possible way of calling blessed the one who was indeed a living *fiat:* "Be it done to me according to thy word." (Luke 1. 38.) What Christ said in fact was, "Whoever hears the word of God and keeps it is my mother" (see Luke 8. 21), and here, of course, he states the perfect truth—Mary is the prototype of the Christian life of faith. Fr. Braun's *loi de Séparation*[22] seems to me to imply something much more profound than a mere confirmation of the priority of spiritual ties over those of blood relationship. This deeper significance is to be found in Christ's ontological situation.

[21] Various attempts have been made to divest Jesus' question: "Woman, what is that to me and to thee?" (John 2. 3–4) of the implication that Jesus is putting a distance between himself and his Mother, but every exegete has eventually to go back on any such decision. F. M. Braun's phrase is very much to the point: ". . . la transcendance séparante du Fils" (*La Mère des fidèles,* Paris and Tournai [1953], p. 116: see also pp. 51–5.)

[22] Braun, p. 62.

It does certainly appear as though the psychological basis of Mary's religious attitude is one of strength in faith—a hoping against hope, against all the outward signs which seem to contradict this faith. We are all too readily inclined to suppose that Mary's religious strength was achieved in easy circumstances of life. This is, however, by no means the case. How is it possible to imagine that she met with no difficulties in her religious life? This does not necessarily mean that the holiness of a person's life is directly related to the degree of drudgery and toil in that life. Nor should we infer, on the other hand, that the holy life is entirely without difficulties and heavy burdens. Mary, it is true, did not experience any of the difficult conflicting impulses which commonly assail sinful human nature, but her refined spiritual nature—the result of her immaculate conception—made her infinitely more sensitive and receptive, as Christ was in the Garden of Olives. Her immaculate state did not, however, make it possible for her to escape from the fact that she was living in a sinful world which was predisposed to misunderstanding. She too was exposed to all those incalculable and irrational elements common to the human situation—the coming together of inexplicable circumstances, the machinations inherent in communal life, the senseless and harsh conflict of human passions—all of which can lead to the brutal oppression of a totally innocent person. Mary was no exception to this "normal" human situation by virtue of her immaculate state, but it did clearly bestow on her a special power which, though it did not diminish the pain of the situation in which she found herself, certainly enabled her to experience it, in her complete submission to God, in a totally different way.

We do well to envisage the family at Nazareth as people engaged in a struggle for their faith, bravely facing all life's difficulties in their complete surrender to God's supreme rule. The true and complete picture of Mary's life is not to be found in the apocrypha of the New Testament, but in the sober account of the Gospels. Her life does not follow the pattern of a fairy-tale, like that of Snow-White. No little forest birds hold her clothes in their beaks and carry her away out of reach of danger to the accompaniment of sweet, heavenly music. If this were so, she would not be an example of strength for us in our day-to-day struggle with the harsh realities of a life which is anything but a fairy-tale. She would simply be a narcotic, and we should wake up after the effects had worn off to face the stern reality of life with a feeling of inconsolable dreariness even more powerful than before. Mary's life was, like ours, truly human, and she was also involved in the same sort of oppressive, hopeless and often apparently insoluble social situations in which every human being is at some time or another placed. But she showed us, by her example, how faith in the mystery of the living God is stronger than human life, stronger, too, than death—even the death of her own Messiah.

It is possible to sum up Mary's religious life in this way. Revelation is more than a mere communication of truth or knowledge. It is at the same time a saving event which must be constantly regarded with love and actively experienced in and through faith, so that one may penetrate the mystery of this revelation, gradually unfolding though always veiled. Mary provides us with a sublime example here. She is the prototype, the very first example of a truly Christian sacramental life of faith. She was deeply involved and fully implicated in the visible events of Christ's human life in the world. Because of this she rose to accept, in faith, the divine mystery which was made visible, and indeed public, in the outward "sacramental sign" of Christ's humanity, and allowed herself to be bathed in the strength which came to her from the grace of his humanity. Her strong faith and trust enabled her to penetrate Christ's human "shroud" and enter a divine world. The mystery of Mary's religious life and holiness is to be found in her faith, hope and charity. Scripture gives us very few facts concerning Mary's life and throws only occasional glimpses of light on the concrete picture of her faith in its gradual growth towards this ultimate victory, and thus of her sacramental life. But what we do in fact know is sufficient for us to be able to give her the title, "Queen of Confessors."

THE KEY TO
THE SECRET OF MARY'S RELIGIOUS LIFE

We do not have to look very far to find the key to Mary's holiness, since she herself proclaimed the secret of her life in her answer to Gabriel. She is the *handmaid* of the Lord. This word is charged with Old Testament spirituality. The *doulia,* or "service" of God—to be God's servant or handmaid—in the Old Testament stands for the synthesis of a life dedicated to God, though we must be careful to observe the particular shade of meaning with which the words are used. Yahweh is the Sovereign Monarch who created everything and who directs and guides his creation according to his pleasure. The "servants of Yahweh" (the original was in fact "slaves of Yahweh," though the word excluded, in this context, any reference to the disgrace of the slave's status) were the pious Israelites who accepted God's sovereign majesty, fully embodied it in their lives and placed themselves completely at God's disposal. Mary's declaration that she is the handmaid of the Lord is strictly in this tradition. It affirms her complete dependence upon God's pleasure and her readiness to place herself entirely at God's disposal. The wonderful mystery of Mary consists in this—that, firmly convinced that she was God's "property," she was completely open to the mystery of God. In confessing that she was Yahweh's handmaid, Mary exposed the depth of her religious soul. We can best appreciate the full depth of this reality by relating the concept of the "handmaid of the Lord" to the substance of the Magnificat, from which Mary emerges as one of the *anawim* or *ebyonim*—the "poor of Israel." The *anawim*—Yahweh's poor, the servants of God, those who fear God—are those who, in their lowliness, place all their trust in God. Later they become identified with the "remnant of Israel" who were to inherit God's kingdom. (It should be noted that these *anawim* were as a rule not held in high esteem in the world—this is in fact the origin of the Old Testament concept of "poverty," which with the passage of time came to have a more and more religious connotation.) Israel itself eventually became the "poor one of the Lord."[23]

The post-exilic books of the Old Testament especially are marked by the spirituality of the *anawah,* the poor and lowly servant. The *anawim* are the quiet folk who "fear God." Psalm 34 (33), for example, is itself a psalm of a "poor man" (*v.* 7). The poor are those who seek refuge in the Lord (*v.* 5, 11). They are God's saints (*v.* 10), the just (*v.* 16, 20, 22), whose life on this earth is not particularly happy, but who, despite the humiliations which they are called upon to endure, remain the trusting and faithful servants of Yahweh (*v.* 23). Their spirituality amounts in fact to this, "Be subject to the Lord and pray to him" (Ps. 37 (36). 7), for "they that wait upon the Lord shall inherit the land" (*v.* 9). They are, finally, the "faithful," in the strictly biblical sense of the word—they *believe* unconditionally in God. They are, in the religious sense, the backbone of the Jewish people. Their counterparts are the "arrogant," the "proud," the "wicked" who trust in themselves, the self-centred people who do not understand the meaning of religious humility. These are the people who, no doubt, have a good time in this world. The poor of Israel, however, rejoice, because Yahweh "will exalt the *anawim* unto salvation" (Ps. 149. 4) and humble the proud. The publican who humbly beats his breast is the "poor man" of the Old Testament. The Pharisee, on the other hand, who in his self-glorification stands in the front, is a "proud man."

Christ himself epitomized the spiritual attitude of the *anawah* in the Sermon on the Mount. He referred to the "poor in spirit," the "meek," the "merciful"—expressions which indicate the full range of the Hebrew *anaw* (poor, in the religious sense, humble). It is these who, according to Christ, and indeed according to the Old Testament, are open to receive the Kingdom of God. (Matt. 5. 3.) They are the "poor in spirit" (*v.* 3), the "meek" (*v.* 4),

---

[23] A great deal has been written about this concept of *anawah* (poverty-lowliness). Perhaps the best, or at least the most provocative, contribution is that of A. Gelin, *Les Pauvres de Jahvé,* Paris, n.d. (Témoins de Dieu, no. 14).

"they that mourn" (v. 5), "they that hunger and thirst after justice" (v. 6), the "merciful" (v. 7), the "clean of heart" (v. 8), the "peacemakers" (v. 9), "they that suffer persecution" (v. 10), those who are reviled and persecuted for Yahweh's sake (v. 11)—these are all the Old Testament variations of meaning contained in the concept of the *anaw,* the poor man (in the religious sense), the little one, or lowly one of God.

In the same context of *anawah,* Christ, in the words of St. Luke, rejoicing in the Holy Ghost, thanked the Father for having revealed all this (that is, the meaning of the Kingdom of God) to the "little ones." (Luke 10. 21.) The sign which Christ gives of the advent of the Kingdom of God is that "the poor have the Gospel preached to them." (Matt. 11. 5.) He goes even further than this by revealing himself to his disciples as the Poor One in person— "learn of me, because I am *anaw,*" that is, meek and humble of heart. (Matt. 11. 29.) This concept of poverty thus becomes the definition of Christian religiosity. Christ himself "being rich, became *anaw* [poor]" (see 2 Cor. 8. 9), "emptied" and "humbled" himself (Phil. 2. 7. 8)—became the perfect realization and embodiment of religious humility. Already the Old Testament had, however, prophesied that the Messiah would come in this form. The idea of the *Ebed Yahweh,* the "Servant of God," the "Suffering Servant" figure, the "poor one of Yahweh," runs through the Old Testament, at first personified in Israel, the "holy remnant," but later identified, in the Prophetic Books, with the person of the Messiah himself. (See Isa. 52. 13–53. 12.)[24]

To return to Mary's attitude, her reaction to the Annunciation and the whole of the Magnificat are permeated with this spirit of *anawah*—"He hath regarded the *poverty and lowliness* [*anawah*] of his *handmaid*" (Luke 1. 48), "He hath put down the mighty . . . but hath *exalted the poor* and lowly" (v. 52), "He hath filled the *destitute* with gifts and the rich he hath sent empty away" (v. 53), "He hath taken pity on Israel, his *servant*" (v. 54), ". . .

[24] See R. J. Tournay, "Les Chants du Serviteur dans la seconde partie d'Isaïe," in *RB,* 59 (1952), pp. 355–84, 481–512.

his *mercy* . . . is upon them that fear him" (*v.* 50). All Israel's religiosity, based on this notion of *anawah* and expressed as an utter trust in God the Helper and Redeemer, flows together in Mary's spiritual attitude. She is Israel personified, the "poor one of Yahweh" raised up by him. "Behold the handmaid of the Lord" —these words express a living act of faith made at God's decree. Christ is the "Servant of Yahweh." In communion with him, Mary is the "Handmaid of the Lord." In this she reveals her complete humility before God, her quality of pure receptiveness and her desire to conceive his Son.[25]

In addition to the idea of poverty, another shade of meaning is contained in Mary's answer to Gabriel. The phrase "servant [handmaid] of the Lord" sometimes has a very special meaning in the Old Testament. The Patriarchs, the Prophets and the great religious leaders of the Chosen People—Abraham, Moses, Joshua, David and so on—are given the special title of "servants of the Lord."[26] They are men of God with a particular religious mission assigned to them by God. The whole of their lives is dedicated to the service of God. Mary's words signify that she accepts, in the same spirit, but with a far greater degree of receptiveness, her mission from God—to become the mother of the royal Messiah. Though she is, in her humility, unaware of their implication, these words constitute a declaration that she is already the queen of the patriarchs and prophets.

In the first place she called herself the "handmaid of the Lord" and then replied, in answer to God's offer, "Be it done to me according to thy word." She did not, it should be noted, reply, "Yes, I will. I accept." She was clearly aware that what was about to happen was not to be brought about by human means, but was

---

[25] It should not be forgotten that, when she spoke these words, Mary was still in the period of her betrothal and had not yet been solemnly led, as a bride, into the house of her bridegroom. (Matt. 1. 18.) This implies that, according to Jewish custom, she was at that time only about fourteen years of age!

[26] See *Doulos, doulia* in Kittel, *Theologisches Wörterbuch zum Neuen Testament,* Vol. II, Stuttgart (1935), pp. 264–82 (Rengstorf).

purely the work of grace, and that the task which was implied in it—her ensuing motherhood of the Child she was to conceive—was a divine commission. A reply such as "Yes, I accept" seemed to her to be too ambitious. Indeed, to be more exact, it simply did not occur to her to reply in such a way. In mystic simplicity, she merely said—"May it be so," or "May it be accomplished in me." In this, Mary showed her absolute receptivity, her completely free and open attitude—"He who is mighty has accomplished great things *in* me."

We now know, from our examination of the Gospel account, how the secret of Mary's religious life can best be understood. We know too how Mary herself formulated this secret. Finally, it is possible to discover, from Scripture, how Christ, who lived for years in the closest intimacy with his mother Mary, has revealed to us the essence of her holiness—though here it is necessary to read between the lines. When Christ, in the Sermon on the Mount, repeatedly called the *anaw,* the poor, blessed in the eight Beatitudes, he did not have any abstract Christian ideal in mind. He had already experienced the concrete realization of this ideal, in the house in Nazareth, in the persons of Mary and Joseph.[27] The "eight" Beatitudes, inspired by the Holy Ghost, are not unattainable Christian ideals. They constitute Christ's canonization of his mother Mary and of all who live according to her example.

"Blessed are they that suffer persecution" (Matt. 5. 10)—and who have to flee from their homes, just as Mary, for the sake of the Justice which was Christ, was forced to seek refuge in Egypt; "Blessed are they that mourn" (*v.* 5), like Mary, who looked in sorrow for the divine Child she had lost (Luke 2. 48); "Blessed are the merciful," who try to help a family in need, as Mary did

[27] We have already drawn attention to the connection existing between the "poor one of the Lord" and "handmaid of the Lord" and the "meek and humble of heart" who are blessed. Lagrange has already suggested that there may be an interdependence between the Sermon on the Mount and Mary's attitude. The Protestant theologian, A. Asmussen, has taken up this idea and developed it more fully in his book, *Maria, die Mutter Gottes,* Stuttgart, 1950.

at Cana, even by asking for a miracle; "Blessed are the poor and lowly of heart," for God will look down upon "the lowliness of his handmaid" (Luke 1. 48, Magnificat), as he did upon Mary; "Blessed are the meek," who, like Mary when she could find no shelter in Bethlehem at the time of Christ's birth, do not become rebellious, for "they shall possess the land" (i.e., everything) (v. 4); "Blessed are they that hunger and thirst after justice"[28]—those who wait patiently, like Mary, for the fulfilment of Israel's expectations—for "they shall have their fill" (v. 6). This list of blessings is in fact a detailed amplification of the ancient psalm: "Yahweh will exalt the *anawim* unto salvation." (Ps. 149. 4.) Mary became the Mother of the Justice whose coming Israel had awaited for so long.

Many people will be reminded here of the "spiritual childhood" of the little St. Thérèse: "Suffer the little children to come unto me . . . for of such is the Kingdom of God." (Mark 10. 14.) In her *anawah,* her poverty and lowliness, Mary regarded herself as the least of all human beings, and for this reason she is the greatest in the Kingdom of Heaven: "Whosoever shall humble himself as this little child, he is the greater in the Kingdom of Heaven." (Matt. 18. 4.) It is noteworthy, too, that the Holy Ghost, who overshadowed the whole of Mary's life, is called the *Pater pauperum,* the Father of the lowly, in the *Veni Creator.*

This outline of Mary's religious attitude is the best way of approaching the mystery of her life and the dogma of this particular religious reality.

In the Message the angel said, "The Lord *is* with thee." The priest, turning towards us during Mass, says to us, *Dominus vobiscum,* "May the Lord be with you." He prays that this may be so, since there is always some corner of our heart where God is still not made welcome. In many important aspects of our lives we are still "without God"; our hearts are still, in part, unredeemed and we are not both inwardly and outwardly complete Christians. But Mary was told, "The Lord *is* with thee," and there was no

[28] This is a typical expression of the messianic expectations of Israel.

single aspect of her human heart, no single part of her body which was estranged from the living God. She belonged entirely to God —"Behold the handmaid of the Lord."

God was with Mary. This was her grace. But grace is always accompanied by a commission. In Mary's case the exquisite grace, "the Lord is with thee," went together with her sublime commission, to be with the Lord, and she fulfilled this commission in a sublime manner. When she conceived Christ it was not simply a question of the living God, the Lord, coming to her. She also went to him, the "Christ" for whom she had been waiting for so long —her conception was a religious ascent to the Messiah. Thus, in Mary, the Incarnation took the form of a living encounter between God the Redeemer and mankind waiting for the Messiah. Christ came too to those who shared Mary's faith, but "his own received him not" (John 1. 11), because they had not been waiting for him in their hearts. Mary was all expectation and longing for the God who was to come, and this is why she received him when he actually came. Her longing anticipated the reality of this loving encounter in her heart and her womb because God was already with her from the very first moment of her existence. Mary's intimacy with God was so close that God, in his nearness to her, was able and ready to become man, as flesh of her flesh. It was pure love-in-faith which brought about Mary's motherhood. God gave his love to her and she, giving love in return for his love, became the Mother of the God-man Christ in love and faith. From this moment Mary grew so intimately together with Christ that his actions became hers too, though their ways were different.

Our task in the following chapter will be to attempt to analyse this delicate reality—the growth of a mother in her Child's life and work.[29] It is inevitable that any such analysis will to some extent misrepresent the image of the Mother of Christ in its original

[29] Scripture, of course, supplies us with the starting-point for our consideration of the mystery of Mary. In this context I should like to draw attention to my essay "Exegese, Dogmatik und Dogmenentwicklung" in *Exegese und Dogmatik,* ed. H. Vorgrimler, Mainz (1962), pp. 91–114.

fullness. An examination of this kind is, however, necessary, and it can at the same time yield very useful results, so long as care is taken to refer back continually to the original image and each detailed aspect is constantly viewed against the background of the concrete, living reality that Mary is Christ's and our mother.

2

MARY'S PLACE
IN THE HISTORY OF REDEMPTION

IN ORDER TO APPRECIATE the universal significance which Mary
has for us in the order of salvation, it is necessary to place her
role in its proper perspective. First and foremost, we should never
lose sight of the fact that she is, like us, a *redeemed* human being.
The sublime position which she occupies as one redeemed through
Christ is closely connected with her motherhood of Christ and
of all human kind. In stressing the fact that she is redeemed, we
are in fact paying homage. It is necessary for us to consider first
of all the exceptional manner of Mary's personal redemption, at
the same time neglecting to some extent the consequences for the
whole of humanity of this special state of redemption. If this is
done, it should be possible, at a later stage, to throw even more
light on these implications and to view in a truer perspective the
knowledge of faith which the Church possesses about the total
significance of Mary in the redemption brought by her Son.

MARY'S PERSONAL REDEMPTION: THE OBJECTIVE
GIFT AND THE PERSONAL APPROPRIATION OF IT

Definition of "Objective" and "Subjective"
Redemption

Because of the various meanings associated with the terms "objective" and "subjective" redemption and in view of their impor-

tance in any discussion as to whether Mary is or is not Christ's active partner in the "objective" redemption, it is necessary to define these terms in accordance with their theological significance. It is important here that our approach should not be arbitrary, but along lines which seem to us to conform objectively to what we know of our faith.

Redemption is an act of the saving God, who is himself both salvation and redemption. It is an exclusively divine act of salvation. It takes the concrete form of a saving act of God in his humanity—of Jesus Christ, who was both God and man. God became man in order that his divine activity of redemption should be accomplished in humanity. God himself acts personally as a human being, and we are redeemed in and through the human acts of God, the Word. In view of the fact that the God-man is, by reason of his vocation, the representative of the whole of mankind, the mysteries of his human life also have a representative value for the whole of mankind.

What is meant by "objective redemption," then, is the consummation of the redemption of human kind in Christ as head of the human race. The whole of humanity is already redeemed, not only through Christ and his "active redemption" (that is, redemption as an activity which redeems us), but also in him, as the representative of the whole of fallen humanity. The objective redemption is therefore not a reality that lies somewhere *between* Christ and ourselves, and which consequently might be accomplished by another (Mary, for example). Christ himself is Redemption, he *is* grace. This is what we are to understand by "objective redemption." As a result of this, objective redemption is, so to speak, the counterpart to the objective fact that *in* Adam the stain of original sin clings to mankind. *In* Jesus, as our head, the redemption of mankind is an established fact. Not only is the universal cause by which redemption came about firmly established, but the result too—our state of being redeemed—is equally a fact, at least in him who died for our sakes and was resurrected by the Father so that we might live. In "one of ours," and as the first-born of the human religious community, humanity is already reconciled with the Father. According to St. Paul, *we* ourselves are already sitting at the right hand of the Father, that is to say, in the man Jesus Christ—our "type," in whom what has subsequently to be wrought in us has already been accomplished. "Objective redemption" therefore does not refer simply to the redemptive activity completed in the man Jesus, but also to mankind's state of being redeemed in Christ, its head.

"Subjective redemption" in the widest sense means, on the other hand, that what has been brought about in Christ is also actually realized in our lives. What is already an accomplished reality in Christ, as our head, overflows into us. Briefly, it is our actual vital union with Christ.

There are, however, two aspects to this subjective redemption. It is first of all a gift of the God-man, an act of the redeeming Christ, to and in us. This is, so to speak, the objective aspect of our subjective state of redemption. At the same time, subjective redemption is a human and personally free consent to objective redemption and to this gift of God. The two aspects of "subjective redemption," then, are the objective gift and our self-appropriation of this gift subjectively.

It is, however, quite possible that these two aspects of subjective redemption will not coincide chronologically. It can happen that a person is *really* placed in a redeemed situation before he in fact personalizes this real condition of existence by his own personally religious activity. What is in Christ already a fully accomplished fact is realized in embryo in such a person by means of sanctifying grace. This particular form of subjective redemption is sometimes termed a state of being objectively redeemed,[1] and an example of this state is that of the baptized but not yet fully grown child, who is in reality a redeemed child of God, though still according to the measure of childhood. In other words, the grace of redemption is a pure state which has, however, not yet developed into a personal, free and intimately personalized possession by means of an *act* of

[1] This should not be confused with "objective redemption."

divine virtue. This applies to our Lady at the moment of her immaculate conception.

In the fullest sense of the word, subjective redemption implies this redeemed state extended to include man's personally active life. If, then, objective redemption implies that God continues, in spite of everything, to love us, who are sinners, in Christ, subjective redemption similarly implies that we, as free beings, are bound to reciprocate this love by personally loving God—it implies that we are to enter freely, through faith, hope and charity, into what is already a fact in Christ's sacred humanity and thereby to become living members of the body of Christ, our head.

What is meant, then, by "subjective redemption" is our own realization in ourselves of what has already been accomplished in objective redemption, that is to say, in Christ, *as our head*, risen from the dead. This subjective redemption, or share in Christ, may be realized in us in a childlike manner, or it may be realized in a consciously personal manner. The difference between the two is to be found in the irregular psychical development of man, who is involved in Jesus' plan of redemption through the grace of God—either as a redeemed child or as a redeemed person (in the sense of a person who has reached the stage of consciously personal life). At a more profound level it also points on the one hand to the objective gift of subjective redemption, and on the other to the human personalization of this gift. If, then, a man is incorporated into Jesus as a child, with the result that subjective redemption is brought about in him, the subjective appropriation of redemption forms, according to the stage of personal development he has reached in his life, a free assent both to Jesus' objective redemption and to his state of grace, which up to that point has been childlike. In other words, his vital union with Christ becomes, at that point, a personal involvement on his own account.

The state of being redeemed, therefore, is, in the full sense of the word, both a pure, universally effective gift of love on the part of the God-man who alone is capable of sanctifying man, and at the same time a free reception on the part of man. No personal being

ever submits passively to redemption. Redemption never attacks us
by surprise, but is always actively received by us. In this sense the
state of "being redeemed" always contains an element of human
co-operation—man freely consents to receive the redemption which
only the God-man Christ can bring. Thus each individual man is,
with regard to his own redemption, already his own "co-redeemer."
This subjective, personal appropriation of objective redemption, in
other words, of that which is already an established fact in Christ,
is one moment of the whole of God's plan of salvation. The redemption which Christ brings is thus a redemption to which the recipient,
man, freely consents in living faith, strong hope and submissive
love. The human response to his free gift which God demands is the
free gift of man himself. Subjective redemption, especially when it
reaches the stage of perfection in human experience, is the ultimate
goal of objective redemption. The individual shares in the Redemption according to the extent of his free consent to the objective gift of
redeeming grace. In this sense he is a "co-redeemer" with Christ.
Qui creavit te sine te, as St. Thomas says, with St. Augustine, *non
redimit te sine te*: "Created without our intervention, we cannot be
personally redeemed without our co-operation." But our co-operation is contained in the very gift of the redeeming God. Hence it
is possible for us to say that Christ is indeed universally effective,
but not exclusively effective, in the matter of redemption. Objective
and subjective redemption are two aspects of the single redemption
brought to the world by the God-man Christ. Whatever any redeemed man may achieve, however great or small it may be, he
must gratefully attribute to the saving deeds of God made man, for
"God indeed was in Christ, reconciling the world to himself." (2
Cor. 5. 19.)

The Universality of Original Sin

Dogma teaches us that Mary was born in grace, as the Immaculately Conceived. Up till now it has not yet been solemnly defined
that she is nevertheless a redeemed human being. Yet this is implicit

in the doctrine concerning her exclusion from original sin. What is more, religious tradition as a whole confirms that she too was redeemed.

In recent years theologians have devoted a great deal of attention to the study of the exact nature of Mary's state of redemption. Particular attention has been paid to the central problem of Mary's debt to original sin (*debitum peccati originalis*). What precisely is meant by the statement that Mary, as a child of Adam, ought by rights to have contracted original sin? Is she an exception to the universal law of original sin, or is she governed by it, although enjoying special privilege and dispensation? This is by no means a purely academic question, for the nature of her sanctity is changed substantially, according to the answer which we give to this question. For this reason, it is essential thoroughly to investigate this problem.

To come to a deeper understanding of original sin, or the universal solidarity of human kind in sin, within the mystery of faith, it would appear to be sufficient to make a direct and formal appeal to the unity of the human race which is inherent in man's common biological descent; that is to say, to have recourse to the fact that the first man contained the whole of humanity physically in himself. Certainly this aspect cannot be ignored, and it may well emerge at a later stage. But it does not constitute the formal aspect of the problem. There is a tendency to refer to "human nature" as if it were equivalent to a natural thing or animal, for which the individual is regarded simply as being at the service of the full realization of the species of the race. Such beings are not persons—they have merely been produced from ancestors, and are the outcome of the process of reproduction.

A human being is, however, formally a spiritual being. That is why the Church stresses the fact that the soul comes into existence by means of a direct act of divine creation. The person, however, allows the body to share in his personal existence, with the result that what arises from the process of procreation becomes, through the creation of the soul, my personal and human body. The unity of the human community is consequently to be found on a spiritual level, it is the unity of a personal community, a society of persons. The biological community forms merely the substructure of this personal community.

But the unity of a community of persons as such can exist only in the unity of its spiritual values—in the unity of aim, life-destiny and vocation. This unity is at the same time a commission, and reality which calls for fulfilment.

Without going into a detailed theological examination of the whole subject, it is nonetheless necessary to give an outline of the basic aspects of original sin. Adam is, by reason of his vocation, the religious ancestor or representative of the whole human race. The mystery of original sin can be understood only if it is viewed in the context of Adam's representative function within the perspective of the call to all men which unites them to each other. Adam was personally offered original grace. The reason for this was that he, as the head of the human race, should possess the source or fountain-head of grace (*gratia capitis*). God put the religious destiny of the whole of humanity into the hands of one man. It is a question here, then, of a mediator of grace. In offering a fountain-head of grace to Adam, God appointed him to the position of mediator of grace for the whole of mankind. Grace was given to Adam as the source of grace for others. His acquiescence, his consent to this grace, would imply salvation for all mankind. His refusal of this grace, his sin—his refusal to undertake the mediation of grace, his loss of this grace as the source of grace for others—betoken the loss of salvation and consequent disaster for mankind.

What emerges from this, then, is that it is possible to understand the nature of original sin only with reference to its supernatural perspective. Original sin is unthinkable within the context of the purely natural order, since a person who is alien to me is incapable of placing me in a *state* of guilt through no personal fault of my own. In view of the fact that grace is a gratuitous gift on the part of God, it follows that God is also able to define the modality and the measure of his gift of grace according to his wise pleasure. His plan is to give grace to all men in and through the responsible, moral and religious act of grace, that is to say, in and through the mediation of grace of one man. This he accomplishes through Adam as a prelude (which in fact turned out negatively) and through Christ as perfect fulfilment. What God desires is a communion, or community, of saints of the type of a "mystical body," bound together by one single mediator of grace. His aim is to build up and extend the unity of this human community of persons around one single human being.

It is exactly in this task, *as a mediator of grace*, that Adam failed culpably. The source of grace which was offered to mankind in Adam was lost by his representative misdeed and the human race was thereby deprived of this supernatural vocation, binding on all men and promising to make them one within this community. Nothing can be drawn out of a spring that has dried up! In this way the whole of humanity found itself deprived of grace—in a state of absence of grace, or, in the literal sense, of dis-grace with regard to God. Human existence thus became an existence doomed to death, an existence without any inward prospect, an existence which had focused itself of its own accord upon religious failure and all the consequences of this failure. As a result of this, whenever a man appeared in the world, he entered a world of human beings in which he, as man, was not in a true, God-willed relationship with God and in which he was unable to realize his personal vocation—if there were no Redemption! Through his representative deed, which was in a concrete sense a misdeed, Adam won for himself a fallen humanity: "All men lost innocence in Adam's transgression" (*DB*, 793): "By one man sin entered into this world" (Rom. 5. 12): "By the disobedience of one man many were made sinners" (Rom. 5. 19).

Thus it is only bearing in mind Adam's vocation as the mediator of grace that we can fully appreciate the dogma which informs us that there is a causal connection between Adam's sinful act and the sinful state to which the unredeemed person is in a concrete sense subject, even before he personally commits a sinful act. The dogma does not inform us explicitly how this causal link is in fact established. We have endeavoured to do this, not, however, by examining formally the proposition that Adam is the "physical head" of the human race, nor by investigating the proposition that he is the "juridical head" of mankind, but by approaching the question from the position to which God appointed Adam as the mediator of grace by vocation within his plan of salvation. This vocation is not a juridical decree by means of which God intended to hold us all jointly responsible *in* Adam's act. Such a view must present itself to the human mind as highly improbable. But, when Adam was given the chance to be the source of grace, he became, inwardly and in a real sense, the representative of all men, and he was given the commission of mediator of grace. It is only when it is seen in this perspective that original sin can be seen as a mystery that does not present an inner contradiction to the human mind and which nonetheless remains a true mystery without our having to add to it any supplementary mystery of purely human contriving. The sinfulness of our situation is an inward, real sinfulness, but only by reason of Adam's personal guilt. Our sinfulness is a real *state* of sin in us, since from the very beginning our spiritual will is in a situation which is in direct contradiction to the holy will of God, that is to say, a graceless situation which brings in its train those further, inwardly disrupting human consequences which we do not, however, propose to discuss here.

The biological unity of the human race cannot, therefore, explain original sin in its formal aspect. This certainly does not mean to say that this biological unity has nothing to do with the case. This question, it is true, was not dogmatically defined by the Council of Trent, either implicitly or explicitly. Nonetheless, the Council Fathers and the whole of ecclesiastical tradition recognized that there is a connection between monogenism and original sin.[2] One might draw the following parallel: The hypostatic or personal union of Christ is the basis of the fact that it was precisely he

---

[2] See, among other instances, *DB*, 795-6, 788-9, and the papal encyclical *Humani Generis*.

who was, through his divine and real vocation, appointed as representative of the whole of the human race—fallen, yet to be redeemed—so that the fullness of grace, which he possessed by his very nature, was destined to become the source of grace for all other men. In the same way, the fact that Adam is the biological ancestor of the whole of humanity, as a race, is the natural basis for *his* being appointed, by a gratuitous vocation, as the mediator of grace or religious head of the whole of mankind. Furthermore, this is also anthropologically explicable by the fact that man belongs to a species, or race, by reason of his corporeality. The living and corporeal being is, by nature, an individual member of a species, coming into being essentially by birth within the one species. (If this were not the case, the question as to whether we have to do with the *same* species could not be solved.) The first ancestors of this particular species form the origin of the whole subsequent species. On this plane, the ancestors are perpetuated in each individual member of their species. Even if the human species is formally different on account of man's spirituality, this living corporeality is still a valid and true aspect of humanity. As a living corporeality which comes into being essentially by descent, the human person, in assuming this biological corporeality, is closely connected with the whole species and therefore, in a special sense, with the ancestors of the whole race. For, at that level, the coming into being of the first man and woman constitutes the origin of the whole human race, with the result that these two ancestors are of unique importance for humankind.

In considering this question, however, it is important not to lose sight of the fact that this biological unity of the human race, should it be proved true, is only the *basis* for the true unity of the community of persons, and that the whole human being is formally a totally new reality, created by a direct act of God, and cannot as, formally, a spirit, be traced back to purely biological antecedents. The physical and biological inclusion of the human race in Adam cannot, therefore, explain original sin. But as each individual human person is, by virtue of his own corporeality, intimately connected with all his fellow men and, in a very special and fundamental sense, with his first ancestors, it is clear, from the point of view of the history of man's salvation, why God chose these two ancestors in particular to constitute the religious head of the human race, as a race called to form a personal community with God. These ancestors—the living source of humanity as race —were chosen by God to be at the same time the source of grace, the source of that charity which would enable all men to build up this community.

God freely "permitted" man to be unfaithful to his plan of salvation, in view of the fact that the whole of mankind was to be placed under a new head, the man Jesus.

The Universality of the Redemption

The divine and positive meaning of God's permission of original sin is, in the concrete sense, God's positive redemptive will. The solidarity of the human race with Adam in original sin is only the reverse side of our solidarity with Christ, the Redeemer, in grace. Original sin and redemption are the two sides of the same divine mystery—even though God totally transcends the initiative to sin, which is man's sole responsibility. This single mystery is God's saving will to establish the unity of the human community in intimacy with himself in *one* man, "of whose fullness we all have received." God allowed the divine plan to fail in Adam, but accomplished it definitively in Christ. Negatively speaking, the "first Adam" is the pre-revelation of the "second Adam." The "mystical body" of Adam became in fact a community of sinners—certain medieval theologians even referred to the *corpus mysticum diaboli.* Just as by the fall of one all men were condemned, so by the justice of One many were justified. (See Rom. 5.18.) God remained faithful to his love of man, despite human sin. His faithfulness is the Redemption—he included all men in disobedience—in other words, in sin—so that he might, in the end, have mercy on all men. (See Rom. 11.32.) Certainly he did not use sin as a means. The ultimate mystery of God's permission of sin eludes us, but in the concrete sense it can only be understood with reference to his redemptive will. This is indeed so fundamental to our understanding of the question that several of the Church Fathers could see original sin as a mystery absurd and irritating only—except within the context of redemption.

On account of the "first-Adam" situation, through which the whole of humanity was involved in the same unhappy fate, and because of the "second-Adam" situation, which involved the same human race in one and the same saving destiny, there is, in the concrete sense, no single man in existence who is not closely associated both with the lost vocation of the "first Adam" and at the same time with the acquired potentiality for realization of the abiding vocation of the "second Adam." Put in another way, the human community in personal intimacy with God, or sanctifying grace, is possible since original sin only as redeeming grace. The representative reality of the "first Adam" was irrevocable, but God does not begrudge his gifts; he still calls man to grace.

Since the Fall, then, sanctity for men has always been *redemption*. No single human being can be regarded as exempt from this, but this redeeming grace comprises three fundamental levels of meaning, which clarify the full significance of the Marian mystery.

Christ, the "Representatively Redeemed"

More than once St. Thomas ventures to say that Christ's humanity was "justified" in order to be the source of our sanctification.[3] The fact that Christ was not subject to original sin, and could not be subject to it, is founded in his being—he was God himself in human form. Yet he entered into a humanity which was, by reason of original sin, in a real sense incapable of attaining its destination. Christ, though without sinfulness, so to speak took original sinfulness upon himself, and did this voluntarily. He

---

[3] See, among other passages, *ST,* III, q. 34, a. 3, c ad 3: q. 34, a. 1, ad 3: q. 8, a. 5: q. 48, a. 1: I–II, q. 114, a. 6: *In Evang. Joh.,* I, lect. 10.

adopted that concrete humanity which is signed with the seal of its sinful state—death: "Him, who knew no sin, he hath made sin for us, that we might be made the justice of God in him" (2 Cor. 5.21); God sent "his own Son in the likeness of sinful flesh and of sin" (Rom. 8.3), Christ is "the Lamb of God" who bears "the sin of the world" (see John 1. 29).[4] Christ's incarnation, his becoming man, was, in a concrete sense, a becoming human sin. As the representative of fallen humanity, he received by vocation the commission to realize representatively, like Adam before him, the life-destiny of the human race, though by means of a restoration. He underwent this total experience in and through the whole of his human life, culminating in death. For him it was the expression of his total obedience to and constant union with the Father, and he fulfilled his commission to its ultimate limits. Only then were the man and (in him) all men able to fulfil humanity's life-destiny. This fulfilment is now an indestructible possibility for every human being.

Christ, being without sin, had himself no need of a redemption. He is, however, more than "God-man." In the concrete sense he is God-man as the representative of humanity which is fallen, is to be redeemed and is in fact redeemed through him. As the representative of fallen mankind, he *is* the whole of humanity—not simply in the juridical, but also in the real sense, even though this is possible only at a supernatural level. As the representative—the head—of fallen mankind, he was truly redeemed on his resurrection. It is important to grasp this fact—in the representative sense, Christ *is* humanity, fallen and redeemed. He is the "representatively redeemed." This is precisely what is meant by "objective redemption." If Christ is the representatively redeemed, then we too are, in him, already essentially redeemed in principle.

From within sinful humanity, Christ is the sinless redeeming

---

[4] The Greek word used here is *airein*. This can mean either "to take away" or "to bear." What is meant here is to take something up in order to take it away. The Lamb of God bears or carries sin, takes it upon himself in order to extirpate it.

principle and, at the same time, the representatively redeemed. He is the Redemption which gives, but also receives and accepts in our name. The fullness of grace, which he possesses by virtue of his mediation of grace to men, is, by reason of the religious experience of his human life, culminating in death, truly redeeming grace for us, and consequently first and foremost for himself, as our representative. That is why the whole of tradition teaches that Christ, who was, by his concrete incarnation, appointed by God as the head of the human race, ultimately "merited" this function by virtue of his redeeming human life. Through his life and death he acquired a redeemed human race.

In whatever degree or in whatever way human beings receive grace, this will always be a share in the fullness of the redeeming grace of Christ himself, whose grace is representative for us all.

Mary's Redemption by Exemption

It is at once clear from the foregoing that Mary's immunity from original sin does not exempt her from the Redemption. However, her situation differs from Christ's in that the fact that she was not subject to original sin was not due to herself, but to Christ. This distinction means that her redemptive grace has a very special character of its own, both with regard to Christ's redemptive grace and also with regard to our justification.

What concerns us here is, in the first place, the difference between Mary and Christ in this respect. For Mary, the "debt to original sin" is no abstraction, even though what is meant by it is frequently expressed in a hypothetical formula, as, for example, "Mary would have incurred original sin if God had not bestowed a special privilege upon her." This hypothesis, however, overlooks the essential element of the concrete mystery of Mary—that she was in fact elected. This is no abstraction, and cannot be made into an abstraction. It is by presupposing this special conferment of grace, not by trying to ignore it hypothetically, that we have to point out one concrete element of the Marian mystery which makes her *de facto* immaculate existence into a real state of being redeemed. This element is to be found in her true humanity. Mary really belonged to the concrete human community of persons which, on account of the inescapable fact of the first Adam's representative misdeed, became radically incapable of reaching salvation (unless this were made possible by means of a divine act of redemption). Mary's personal membership of that human personal community constitutes, on the religious level, her "debt to sin." Her biological unity with the human race—her descent from Adam—forms no more than the biological substructure and as such cannot formally constitute this *debitum peccati*.

The fact that she did not really incur original sin cannot, therefore, be explained by reference to herself, as in the case of Christ. The "debt" is not something which is extrinsic to her—it affects her very person. Her *de facto* humanity was for her an inward and personal reality. The necessary incurring of original sin was something which was intrinsic to her, and does not only consist in the fact that she entered an objective world of sinful human beings —an objectively sinful situation—although personally exempt from this unhappy plight. The fact that she did nonetheless remain exempt can only be based upon something which is outside herself. This principle can only be found in Christ. The tension which exists between the intrinsic nature of her so-called "debt to original sin" and the extrinsic principle of her *de facto* exemption from original sin leads us to the conclusion that Mary's immaculate state is a redemption by way of exemption or immunity. Her immaculate conception can only be a share in the redemptive grace of the "representatively redeemed," and this occurs, as will emerge later, within her function as the mother of Christ as the head of fallen and redeemed humanity.

The Consequences of This Redemption
by Exemption

Mary was exempt from the universal stain of original sin. What is more, she did not at any time personally commit sin, and indeed was not even acquainted with actual sin or evil desire. This is due entirely to the uniquely sanctifying power of Christ's sacrifice on the Cross, the pure gift of his mercy which is effective in our case in the forgiveness of sins. His mother's sanctity was just as much the result of the shedding of Christ's blood as our feeble efforts to resist sin, or the longing for heaven which the thief on the Cross experienced almost too late. But, with Mary, this goes even further —the mercy and the redemption which she enjoyed were greater and more profound and far-reaching than ours. St. Thomas has observed somewhere that to remain exempt from personal sin, by virtue of God's grace, shows a greater mercy on God's part than to obtain the grace of divine forgiveness for sins already committed. If we consider Christ's redemptive suffering on the Cross in its aspect of sacrificial love, we can, and indeed are bound to, conclude that he suffered first and foremost and most of all for Mary. While he was enduring the agony of the Cross and when he died, Mary, so to speak, occupied the centre of his feelings. As the most beautiful creation of his redemptive death, Mary is the person for whom Christ shed his redeeming blood most liberally and with the most fervent sacrificial love.

In making this assertion, it is important not to lose sight of the special nature of "redemption by exemption." Mary was never a sinner, and this was due only to Christ's redemptive death on the Cross. But, looked at from another perspective, a fundamental difference between her redemption and ours becomes apparent. The malice of sin was never in her, as it was in us. The prevention of sin by anticipation and the forgiveness of sin already committed are both the fruit of redeeming grace. "Redemption by exemption," however, does not include that aspect of expiation which is inherent in a real state of sinfulness. The real distinction between Mary's case—coming redeemed into the world—and ours—being redeemed later—throws a totally different light on the painful character of Christ's death considered as the redemption by exemption of his mother. At the deepest level, Christ's redemption is sacrificing love, a breaking through of God's mercy into a torn and disrupted world which imparted its painful character to this divine intervention. The prevention of the malice of sin by anticipation is indeed in accord with the whole of the Redemption, but it must at the same time be seen in a different light from the expiation of and the redemption from the actually present malice of sin.

On the other hand, however, it is quite true that the "debt to sin" was the curse which was hanging over the whole of mankind and which was a concrete reality in all men, with the single exception of Mary. This constitutes the sublime, unique and exceptional aspect of her real state of redemption. Christ, then, made the painful sacrifice of himself on the Cross in order to remove this universal curse, with the result that Mary too is in reality the fruit of this sacrifice. Even though the assertion that Christ *suffered* most of all for Mary may prove somewhat disconcerting to the theologically informed mind, one can nonetheless maintain this claim, so long as the aspect of great sacrificial love, concretely expressed in Christ's painful death, is stressed rather than the painful character as such of his suffering in the material sense. To express this in another, and perhaps better way, and bearing in mind particularly the *Christian* aspect of the question, Christ's sacrificial love on the Cross was tuned in first and foremost and at the most fervent level to Mary's redemption by exemption. It is only by viewing the question in this way that it is possible to preserve the fundamental truth of Mary's redemption and to avoid isolating her, because of her immaculate conception, from the rest of the human race which has found salvation in Christ alone.

Theologians such as St. Bernard and St. Thomas[5] have indeed played an extremely beneficial and constructive part here, in their denial of Mary's born immaculate state. In so doing, they preserved

---

[5] I shall not go into the discussion as to what was historically St. Thomas's own position. It is undoubtedly true that his denial does not contain the same harsh import as is to be found in many of his followers in the centuries preceding the full development of dogmatic thought on the subject of the Immaculate Conception.

intact the basic Christian view of Mary as a redeemed person, although the possibility of a redemption by exemption[6] did not occur to them. It was only when it was ultimately realized that Mary was in fact a redeemed child of Adam that Duns Scotus was able to formulate theologically the increasing belief in Mary's immaculate state. It was then too that it was realized that the dogma of her immaculate conception ought not to exclude Mary from the normal plan of redemption and situate her outside its framework, as a kind of "extra-Christian" child of paradise. If, then, we consider St. Thomas's denial of the Immaculate Conception not in isolation, simply as a declaration of his own denial, but rather within the framework of the developing dogmatic and historical tradition of ecclesiastical thought concerning the *Immaculata,* it can be seen that his denial emphasizes one primary and indeed fundamental aspect of the Immaculate Conception, namely that Mary is truly redeemed. Following in the tradition of Eadmer, Engelbert, Conrad of Brundelsheim, William of Mare and others, all that Scotus had to add was "by exemption," for the full and real significance of the absence of original sin in Mary to emerge in its precise dimensions as *sublimiore modo redempta,* truly redeemed, but in an exceptional and unique manner.

THE SUBLIME AND EXCEPTIONAL POSITION OF MARY'S PERSONAL REDEMPTION

What we learn from the dogma of the Immaculate Conception, then, is that Mary was, in a real sense, already redeemed from the very first moment of her existence. At no point of her existence was she an unredeemed person—she came into existence as a redeemed human being. She was really redeemed even before she had appropriated her redemption or before she was able to perform a meritorious action. She accomplished this free appropriation of

---

[6] The idea of a grace which prevented particular sins was certainly accepted at that time. Though this is a greater mercy on the part of God, it does not constitute *redemption* (by exemption).

her objectively sublime redemption[7] in the course of the whole of her later free, conscious life of faith, hope and charity. It is possible to compare Mary's state with that of a baptized child. Such a child is already objectively redeemed, but it is only when it matures into a conscious person that it penetrates more and more deeply, as a person, during the whole of its Christian life, into the mystery of the Redemption, and so gradually assimilates, at a more intimate and personal level, the grace of redemption. Mary went through a similar process of development, though without the intervention of sin or sinful desires.

Some theologians maintain that, even while she was in her mother's womb, Mary possessed personal consciousness and, for this reason, was able to accept her redemption subjectively at that stage of her existence. Such a claim is completely without foundation. The privilege of her Immaculate Conception did not in any sense include exemption from the normal process of human development, nor did it imply that she possessed a kind of omniscience, that she was incapable of making any mistakes which were not of a moral nature, or that she was not subject to spiritual progress or improvement, even concerning the mystery of salvation. Like Christ himself, Mary was in no way exempt from the *consequences* of original sin, which she took upon herself, insofar as they were not sinful. Her capacity for suffering and, as we believe, her physical death have, as in the case of Christ, a profound significance within the work of redemption itself.

Even if Mary did personalize her exceptional objective state of being redeemed in a subjectively sublime manner through the whole of her life, it is nonetheless possible to distinguish, in her life as in Christ's, various climaxes which form the summit of her subjective acceptance of Christ's redemption. Chief among these are her virgin openness, her *fiat,* her communion with Christ's

---

[7] It is, however, important to bear in mind here the second meaning of the "state of being objectively redeemed." What we are dealing with in this case is subjective redemption in the manner of a child, that is, the objective gift of a subjective state of being redeemed. The significance of Mary within "objective redemption" proper will be discussed at a later stage.

sacrifice at the foot of the Cross, her physical death and her experience of Pentecost.

Mary, the Exponent of the Old Testament Expectations of the Messiah

Mary's immaculate conception, her exemption from all sinfulness and all wrongful desires, made the unfathomable and pure depth of her loving *fiat* to the Redemption and to her divine motherhood possible. Even before the Annunciation, Mary's subjective redemption had already attained a depth which was beyond the reach of other saints. Yet her holiness of this period was still a "holiness of preparation." Although it was at an incomparably higher level, it was still in the direct tradition of the Old Testament anticipation, the expectant longing for the long-awaited Messiah. Her holiness was the synthesis and the culmination of the longing of the Jews for the coming of the Messiah—a longing which, in its "preparation," was, like the whole of holiness in the Old Testament, a fruit of the redemption which was to come, given in advance of this future redemption. In the immaculate perfection of her eager anticipation of the Messiah who was to come, Mary, though unaware of the greatness which even at that stage was already hers, embodied the whole of the messianic longing of the Jews and brought it to its highest pitch. By virtue of the grace of her exceptional and special election, Mary realized, in her person, the fundamental openness and receptivity of the Old Testament expectation of the Messiah in all its various lines of development, which had been steadily and continuously converging towards one single point. It was this openness and receptivity which became, at least at that level, the ultimate disposition for the Incarnation. All this is, then, the pure work of grace. God prepared for his coming in and through the Jewish people and ultimately through the Virgin Mary. But, as is always the case, every grace is a receiving, from the subject's point of view. Thus, during the whole of the time before the Message, Mary's holiness was a pure receptivity and openness towards God's potential gifts.

It can be no idle fancy or haphazard guess to presume that Mary, by reason of her immaculate state of grace, came to realize in and from the personal experience of her religious life that the inner messianic impulse of her people was rapidly drawing near to its fulfilment. Although the initiative of the Message was certainly from God, there was some element of it which, even before it was uttered, sought a way into Mary's heart. She is for herself a mystery. But there was in Mary an unspoken depth which made her constantly reach out towards the Messiah. Any attempt to deny this is bound to lead to a failure to appreciate the reality of Mary's immunity from original sin from the moment of her conception, a reality which had repercussions on her religious attitude. She felt the Old Testament consciousness of Yahweh's saving acts in Israel to be, so to speak, gathered up in her own person, and she remained thus, though unconsciously and like a question waiting for an answer, "on the look-out."

It is important to situate the problem of Mary's virginity within this context.

Mary's Virginity

Mary's constant virginity, "before, during and after the birth of Christ," is a doctrine of the Church.[8] By virginity, the Church does not merely imply the material fact of a virgin state, but first and foremost a definite spiritual and religious attitude, a fully involved virginity.

This, however, does not mean that there was no development of any kind in Mary's positive attitude towards her virginity. As we have already seen, Mary certainly developed within her immaculate state of holiness. In recent years there has been a marked tendency to accept, from the point of view of biblical exegesis, the possibility of growth in Mary's appreciation of her virginity—the possibility of a development from an Old Testament virginity to a specifically Christian kind of virginity. This certainly goes counter to a long theological tradition, and at first sight it may seem to

[8] The Council of Trent; see *DB*, 993.

be a somewhat disconcerting idea. It would be wrong, therefore, to advocate personal views without due care and diffidence. The decisive elements in this matter must be the Word of God himself —Holy Scripture—and the Church's knowledge of the Faith, in both of which we must be guided by the authority of the Church concerning doctrine. Furthermore, before even attempting to reach a justified understanding of this question, it would be a totally unwarranted presumption simply to deviate at random from the view which for centuries has been so dear to the Christian mind.

An open-minded interpretation of Scripture and a knowledge of the mentality of Palestinian Judaism have, however, gradually succeeded in directing Christian thought towards a definite aspect of Mary's virginity which actually brings out the deepest Christian significance of her virgin state without sacrificing any of its essential value. In the previous edition of this book (1954), I already suggested the possibility of this view, but as long as it could not to some extent be validly proved, it seemed to me to be better not to take my personal preferences and conjectures too much into account. And therefore I still feel constrained to admit, in all honesty, that this new interpretation is open to certain possible objections.

The entire problem is centered in the interpretation of the text "How shall this be done, because I know not man?" (Luke 1. 34.) In my opinion it has not so far been apodeictically proved that this text is bound to be interpreted in any particular way. Some dubious points are certain to remain, whatever interpretation is accepted. At present, however, there are basically three important current interpretations which we must now consider.

(1) The traditional interpretation. Even before the Annunciation, Mary had intended to lead the life of a virgin in her marriage with Joseph. In this case, the question which she put to the angel —"How shall this be done, because I know not man?"—is an obvious and understandable one. Such an interpretation is certainly permissible from the purely exegetical point of view. And, if it is conceivable that a young Jewish girl of that period should ever

intend to lead a virgin married life, then this interpretation should undoubtedly have first claim, from the exegetical point of view. Some biblical scholars, however, maintain that any such promise on Mary's part would be entirely out of the question, in view of the fact that virgin marriage was at that time completely inconceivable to the religious mind of the Jewish community. Certainly all kinds of guesses have been made on this score. On account of the religious and social feelings of the Jewish community, it is true that Mary would only be able to carry out her intention to remain a virgin within the married state. Other scholars assume that Mary's father had no sons and that Mary, as heiress according to the Jewish law (see Num. 36. 6), was consequently virtually obliged to marry, with the result that once again she was only able to realize her intention to remain a virgin within the married state. The other interpretations do not simply attack the possibility of a virgin marriage; they even claim that an intention on the part of a Jewish *girl* to embrace celibacy was quite inconceivable. The fact is that an intention of this kind does to a very great extent contradict all that we know of Old Testament piety. Even for a man, celibacy was most exceptional throughout the history of Israel.

This interpretation, however, has the merit that it does not *a priori,* by reason of extrinsic circumstances, exclude the possibility that Mary formed the intention of remaining celibate during marriage before the Annunciation. That this possibility was excluded *a priori* because of the nature of Jewish spirituality—which Mary undoubtedly inherited—seems to me to imply an undervaluation of God's free choice of his means to save, which in the Old Testament so often took those who believed in him by surprise. It has been said, certainly, that God never acts independently of second causes, and, as far as the human causes are concerned, there is nothing that can possibly point in the direction of celibacy in the case of a young Jewish girl. On the contrary, everything points in the opposite direction. But, if this is so, we are leaving out of consideration the enormous reality which, even if Mary was herself ignorant of her state, we simply cannot ignore—the fact of her immaculate conception and the potentialities inherent in this fact. Mary's immaculate conception is, in any case, a reality which she bore vitally within her and which led her, in her perfect openness towards God, to a state of exceptional receptivity and readiness for complete and active involvement.

There is no need to mention "revelations" in this context— grace can spur the believer on to perform actions which, when viewed within the normal environment of the individual, seem to be absurd and inconceivable. This, indeed, was so in Mary's case *after* the Annunciation, despite her Jewish environment. What emerges, then, is that reasoning based on considerations of Palestinian Jewish society may well be exegetically correct, but that such arguments cannot be regarded as convincing either from the theological point of view or from the point of view of biblical theology, if we bear in mind Yahweh's statement in the Old Testament: "Is there anything hard [= impossible] to God?" (Gen. 18. 14.). What notion can we have, poor sinners that we are, of a soul that was utterly holy and, even in its most remote recesses, truly in love with the living God? We can scarcely hope to grasp God's purpose with the Blessed Virgin by way of speculation or *a priori* exclusions. It is only if we listen attentively to the word of revelation, living in the Church, and thus to Holy Scripture, that we shall ultimately come to learn what this purpose is. What is more, if we do hearken in this way, our minds will also be opened to other possibilities.

(2) A view of another possibility is opened by the second interpretation of the text, which is favoured by many exegetes.[9] The statement: "I know not man" could have a totally different meaning from that ascribed to it by the first interpretation. Before the Mes-

[9] To name a few who tend towards this second view, I quote D. Haugg, *Das erste biblische Marienwort. Eine exegetische Studie zu Lukas* 1. 34, Stuttgart (1938); P. Gaechter, *Maria im Erdenleben,* Innsbruck (1953); A. Roets, "Maria's voornemen tot maagdelijkheid," and "De zin van Maria's maagdelijkheid," Coll. Brug. Gand., 1 (1955), pp. 448–77 and pp. 225–39; R. Guardini, *Die Mutter des Herrn,* Würzburg (1955).

sage, Mary made no promise at all to lead the life of a virgin within the married state. When she married she intended to carry out all that the Jewish law prescribed. It is quite true that she lived the life of a virgin, but, from her legal marriage to Joseph *before* the Annunciation, we may assume that she fully intended to lead a normal married life with Joseph after the wedding, the official cohabitation as man and wife. The Annunciation and the content of the Message, however, made her renounce normal marital relationships for the sake of Christ. The Christian ideal of virginity, therefore, came into being as a direct result of the fact of Christ.

What, then, does Mary's statement "I know not man" really imply according to this interpretation? Its meaning becomes apparent as soon as Mary's actual situation, within the Jewish community and at the time of the Message, is considered. Before the Message she was betrothed, or as we would now say, "engaged" to Joseph. It would, however, be more accurate to say that she was "promised" to Joseph by her father; in the Jewish community this was a formal legal transaction, in which the daughter was in fact handed over to the husband before the Law. This formed a valid marriage, as we understand it in the West, though with one very important distinction—married life and cohabitation as man and wife did not actually commence until after the ceremony during which the bridegroom took his wife home had taken place. Moreover, it sometimes happened that this ceremony was postponed for months after the betrothal or "engagement." Although there was perhaps a certain degree of laxity in Judea, this practice was strictly observed in Galilee especially, and there married relationships were not deemed permissible until after the official ceremony of cohabitation. Between the betrothal and the official cohabitation, then, a state of virginity existed in marriage. In this respect, the Jewish "marriage of betrothal" bears certain similarities to "engagement" in the modern sense of the word.

At the time of the Annunciation Mary was not living with Joseph in his home, and consequently had no marital relationship with him. Her answer to the angel, "I know not man," may therefore have this meaning: "How shall this be done, because I am not yet living with Joseph in his home?" or, expressed in more modern terms, "How is this possible? I am not actually married yet." Mary's answer, therefore, would have meant something like this: "As a girl who is engaged to Joseph, and especially as an engaged girl in Galilee, I am not in a position to be able to become a mother in the near future." The angel's reply is quite straightforward: "You will become a mother without the intervention of a man—as a virgin."

This interpretation is quite plausible from the exegetical point of view. Mary made her decision to remain a virgin throughout the whole of her married life at the time of the Message. It is, however, doubtful whether it is apodeictic. The angel did not give Mary to understand that what was to happen would take place at once. On the premise—and in the case of this interpretation it must be a premise—that Mary's actual married life followed the normal pattern, and that she believed that the prophesied Messiah would come into the world as the result of normal marital relationships, could she not equally well have believed that the Message would only be fulfilled after—perhaps several months after—her official cohabitation with Joseph as man and wife? It is all too easy to brush aside the difficulty that the promise of motherhood, made in the Message, was to be carried out in the future: "Behold, thou *shalt* conceive in thy womb and *shalt* bring forth a son; and thou *shalt* call his name Jesus." (Luke 1. 31.) It is, of course, true that, in similar messages of heavenly origin, the future tense is frequently used to express something which is actually going to be fulfilled at the precise moment of the message itself. This is even normal to a very great extent, but it is not universally the case. Abraham, for example, was also promised a son by his wife, but his faith in God's promise was put to the test for a very long time indeed! This, then, is what tends to rob this particular interpretation of much of its compelling virtue. Mary's objection, "It cannot be done *now*," becomes extremely problematical, if it will indeed be possible in a few months', or even in only a few weeks', time. In any case, we do not know for how long she was engaged.

(3) Finally we must consider the third interpretation, which, although it leaves certain serious questions unanswered, is nonetheless very attractive.[10] Fr. Audet also takes the view that Mary resolved to remain a virgin during her married life as a result of the content of the Message. Like the exponents of the second interpretation, he too maintains that a virgin marriage in Palestine was quite unthinkable. In his exegesis of the text "I know not man," he stresses the great importance, in this connection, of the Old Testament text, "Behold, the young girl [the virgin] is pregnant, and will bear a son, whom she will call Emmanuel" (Isa. 7. 14: the translation is based on that of the *Bible de Jérusalem*). In the Palestinian Jewish community of that time, the word *almah* meant a young, marriageable girl, and referred to the girl's youth and social status rather than to her virtuousness. Her virginity, in the moral sense, was assumed. It was thus a young marriageable girl who was to become the mother of the Messiah. As one brought up on the Bible Mary was assumed to have been acquainted with this text and to have meditated upon it. This is not based on pure supposition, since it does emerge quite clearly from many instances in the Old Testament that messages of heavenly origin are definitely connected with a certain expectation or "problematic" element in the psychology of specially privileged persons and this, so to speak, seizes hold of the problematic element. From the religious and psychological point of view, this observation seems to me to be of the greatest importance. What is of heavenly origin does not simply overcome a human subject; there is a certain point of contact at the human level. There is, in any case, a striking parallelism between the Message which was announced to Mary and that which was announced to Gideon.[11]

The claim, then, that Mary was engaged in prayerful meditation upon this text when she suddenly heard the angel's voice is not at all far-fetched. She was still a virgin—a "young, marriageable

[10] J. P. Audet, "L'Annonce à Marie," in *RB,* 63 (1956), pp. 346–74.

[11] Judges 6. 11–24. St. Luke's account is also written in the characteristic and classical "Message" style.

girl." The *words* which the angel addressed to her made her turn pale, because she realized at once the full extent and implication of these words—she was to be that very "young, marriageable girl" to whom the Scriptures referred. Mary's reply to the angel is quite intelligible if it is looked at from the point of view of the total concept of messianic motherhood, with reference to the ultimate perspective of the fulfilment of the prophecy of Isaiah and thus of the "virgin motherhood": "How shall this be done, because in that case I know not man—that is to say, because in that case I may, or must, not know a man?"—"in that case" referring to the fulfilment of the prophecy of Isaiah. This interpretation does not in any way force or distort the text from the exegetical point of view.[12] Mary asks for an explanation concerning the Virgin Birth, wondering whether there is perhaps something which she has to do. The angel's reply has a direct bearing upon this question—she is to leave everything to God; the Holy Spirit or the power of God will take care of it, since nothing is impossible to God. As the servant of the Lord, Mary accepts this: "Be it done to me."

This interpretation does appear to have much to commend it. There is, however, one difficulty. This particular prophecy of Isaiah played no part in the rabbinical tradition,[13] with the result that the deeper significance of this text was not understood until after the events in which Mary was involved. In contrast to the other Evangelists, St. Matthew refers explicitly to the Old Testament prophecy. (Matt. 1. 23.) This is certainly a very real difficulty, though not an insurmountable one, in view of the fact that, even without any special "inspiration," Mary was inwardly much more accurately tuned in to Scripture, and thus more capable of a deep understanding or appreciation of it, than the rabbis. There is an incidental and minor difficulty, too, in the angel's reply, in the particular stress which he placed on the fact that with God everything is possible

[12] The Greek word *epei,* "because" or "for," is often used elliptically in Scripture with the meaning of "because in that case."

[13] See Strack and Billerbeck, *Kommentar zum Neuen Testament aus Talmud und Midrasch,* Part I, Munich (1922), pp. 49–50.

and in his allusion to the case of Mary's cousin Elizabeth. This certainly seems to indicate that Mary, for her part, had not thought at all of a virgin motherhood. In this case it would be possible to regard this third interpretation as absolutely convincing only so long as the Virgin Birth, to which the text of Isaiah made a very vague allusion, was already associated in the mind of the Jewish people with the messianic idea. But this has by no means been finally verified. It is true that we cannot *a priori* limit Mary herself in this way. On the other hand, however, it would be equally wrong purely to *assume* that she had an intimate knowledge and understanding of the deeper significance of the Old Testament text!

There is, then, something for and something against all these interpretations.[14] Something, however, tends to make us favour the proposition that the Message itself provides the best insight into the question of Mary's virginity. The first and the third theses assume certain things which are not substantiated. On the one hand, we have the premise that Mary already formed her intention to remain a virgin during her married life *before* the Annunciation, while on the other we have the premise that she understood the full significance of Isaiah's text. Neither of these premises is *a priori* untenable, but, on the other hand, neither can simply be assumed, at least not without a valid starting-point. It is only the second interpretation which does not make a single premise and, what is more, provides a literally permissible exegesis of the text as we know it. So long as the Church, as the custodian of the treasury of the Faith and consequently of Holy Scripture, does not insist on the traditional hypothesis of an intention formed before the Annunciation to remain a virgin in marriage, then it would seem that, apart from those difficulties which we have already discussed at some length, the second interpretation is the most acceptable from the purely exegetical point of view.

[14] There is another, recent proposition which dispenses with all these difficulties. According to this view, the words were not spoken by Mary, but were "composed" by the Evangelist, who made use of the traditional narrative style to stress the fact that Christ was conceived in Mary's virgin womb.

From the theological and dogmatic point of view, too, this second interpretation makes Mary's virginity appear all the more meaningful. Mary placed herself unconditionally at God's disposal, even going against her own earlier ideas with their undeniably holy intentions. In the light of this interpretation, Mary's celibacy, embraced for Christ's sake, gains its fullest and deepest meaning—she decided, as a direct result of the supernatural fact that she was to become the virgin mother of the Messiah, to remain a virgin throughout her marriage, once this marriage had been contracted.

With Guardini, who also inclines to this view,[15] I should, however, like to draw attention to another shade of meaning, to an openness which is implicit in Mary's state of virginity *before* the Message and which is an openness towards her Christian virginity after the Message. Placing a somewhat different emphasis on Guardini's view, with which I nevertheless for the most part concur, one might say that when Mary married Joseph, she looked forward to a normal married life. It is perfectly possible for people of exceptional holiness to form various intentions of doing certain things, but at the same time to have a kind of undefined presentiment that events may turn out quite differently. In the case of a woman who was born holy and immaculate, this vague, unconscious presentiment is all the more likely to be present. Mary was all openness, her very being was a waiting for God. After the Message she was able, so to speak, to say: "So that was what it was!" It is, after all, impossible for us to overlook the fact of Mary's immaculate conception, which is bound to have had an effect upon her religious psychology. Even her marriage with Joseph was, as far as her share in it was concerned, enveloped in a sphere of mystery, full of divine possibilities. Even *before* the Message she was Christ's most beautiful creation, although she was without

---

[15] R. Guardini, *Die Mutter des Herrn*, pp. 31–6. I cannot, however, bring myself to accept Guardini's exegesis of the text: "I know not man." Mary understood the Message to mean that her motherhood of the Messiah was to take place at once. Yet, according to Guardini, she replied, "I do not see any man"—"There is no man present." This is surely rather difficult to swallow!

doubt unaware of this. There was in her, even before the Message, a mystery which was trying to find a way into her heart, the full depths of which only began to reveal themselves, at least in embryo, at the time of the Message.

Mary is, quite simply, a mystery which cannot be approached with the dissecting knife of purely secular understanding. It is quite probable that it was a vague feeling for the mystery that Mary was even before the Annunciation that gave rise to the theological tradition that Mary formed the intention, even before the Message, to enter upon a virgin marriage. Expressed in this way, this may seem to be an inaccurate statement. Nonetheless, by considering the ever-present potentiality in Mary which was reaching out towards an expectation, that is to say, a potentiality which was not merely abstract, but was, so to speak, latent and implied, we may perhaps be able to come to a deeper understanding of the Marian mystery than by pursuing too closely the various modern interpretations, though these may well, from the purely exegetical point of view, have everything in their favour. In so doing, we do not in any way detract from the value of the modern interpretations, for it was as a direct result of the Message that Mary, the virgin, proceeded to the explicit resolve to live out her marriage as a virgin. There is thus, in Mary's state of virginity before the Message, an implied mystery which did not break through until the time of the Message, and was only apparent as a definite attitude in the light of the Message. For Mary's religious sensibility, then, all things became, from that point onwards, a matter of course, and there was no need even to think about it again. Only in this way can we incorporate exegetical interpretation into a theological examination of the subject without doing any injustice to what has already been achieved by exegesis in this sphere. Mary simply said, "I know not man," and thought only of the present moment, leaving the future in God's hands.

If the period between Mary's betrothal and her official cohabitation with Joseph is considered within the context of her religious psychology—her intense preoccupation with the mystery of the

Messiah—we can gain an even deeper insight into the meaning of the Marian mystery, and see more clearly the tensions and potentialities inherent in it. In Israel, marriage itself had a very deep significance—"The inheritance of the Lord are children [sons]; the reward, the fruit of the womb." (Ps. 126. 3; Ps. 127. 1–3; Gen. 33. 5 etc.) It was not at all unusual, in the history of Israel's salvation, for great figures in the Old Testament to experience a miraculous birth. The great canticle of the New Testament, the Magnificat, which celebrates Christ's birth of a virgin, owes its inspiration to Hannah's canticle of praise on the occasion of the miraculous birth of her son Samuel. (1 Sam. 1. 1–11; 2. 1–10.) There are many other examples in the Old Testament of barren women who miraculously gave birth to sons, and these can also be seen as foreshadowing the even greater miracle that was accomplished in Mary.[16] It is, then, extremely likely that Mary, the young married virgin, sensing in the hidden depths of her religious consciousness that the expectation of her people was approaching its ultimate fulfilment, was powerfully reminded of those miraculous births which had occurred from time to time throughout the history of Israel's salvation. It is probable too that the somewhat vague text of Isaiah may well have played a part in this illumination of Mary's mind. Mary grew up in such close contact with the spirituality of the Old Testament that it is impossible to believe that all these facts of salvation history had no effect upon the formation of her mind and spirit. If we link all this up with the fact that her soul was immaculately conceived and moreover raised up by God himself to the reception of the Message, then we find ourselves unable to accept the recent view, that Mary formed the explicit intention simply to lead a normal married life with Joseph, without certain reservations of a subtle, infinitely profound and almost inexpressible nature. Where the facts of revelation are concerned, however, it is certainly not scriptural exegesis which has the final word to say, although it cannot be denied that recent biblical scholarship has made a very valuable contribution to the

[16] See Gen. 17. 17; 18. 11–12; Judges 13. 2–7 etc.

entire subject, by throwing a fresh light upon the traditional view.

Joseph's attitude too would appear to confirm the foregoing. Called a "just man" in Scripture, he resolved to "put Mary away privately" (Matt. 1. 19) as soon as he learned of her pregnancy. Biblical scholars have still not managed completely to overcome this exegetical stumbling-block. All the various interpretations which have so far been suggested give the impression that they are to some degree forced, and even those who advocate one or other of these views seem themselves to be inwardly aware that something is somewhere out of place. Guardini has, however, already put forward an interpretation which is to some extent acceptable (in *Die Mutter des Herrn*, pp. 36–7), and, more recently, Karl Rahner[17] has thrown an even clearer light on this problem and provided an explanation which seems perfectly plausible. At the same time he has also succeeded in situating Joseph within the proper context of the history of salvation, without falling into the near-heresy of modern "Josephinism." Joseph's resolution to send Mary away did not become fully apparent until the moment when he was informed of the supernatural origin of her motherhood. It has been generally assumed that Mary never discussed the matter with Joseph—but this is, of course, pure supposition. Rahner, on the other hand, assumes the opposite and claims that Scripture in fact provides a point of departure for this assumption: "Mary was *found* with child, of the Holy Ghost." (Matt. 1. 18.)[18] Who else could it have been, Rahner argues, but Joseph himself, who found Mary to be pregnant? If Joseph was unaware of the supernatural origin of Mary's pregnancy, then, considered from the point of view of the Jewish conception of righteousness, the "private putting away" of Mary by Joseph, the "just man," is quite incomprehensible.

[17] See his article, " 'Nimm das Kind und seine Mutter,' Zur Verehrung des hl. Joseph," *GL*, 30 (1957), pp. 14–20.

[18] On the basis of the text itself, it is doubtful whether Joseph actually learned from Mary that her conception was "of the Holy Ghost." It is, of course, possible that this phrase was added by the Evangelist. This, however, has still not been finally established.

On the other hand, however, the claim that Joseph found himself face to face with a paradox, but continued to believe in Mary and committed this enigma to God's judgement, without first personally discussing the matter quietly with Mary, is at least unlikely from the psychological viewpoint. The normal course of events is, quite obviously, that Joseph became aware of Mary's pregnancy and talked about it with her. Mary, for her part, told him everything. As her lawful husband, Joseph must have had the right to ask her for an explanation, though it is of course always possible that a presentiment of mystery in the case may have led him, like Mary, to refrain from talking about it. In any case, the reasons for Joseph's decision to send Mary away emerge clearly from the foregoing hypothesis. Once he was acquainted with the origin of this sublime mystery, Joseph was immediately conscious of the fact that he could no longer lay any claim to such a woman. Consequently he retired into the background or, in other words, looked at within the context of the Jewish conception of marriage, he sent Mary away, deciding that he would not live with her. He felt that he was external to this particular event in the history of salvation—that God's hand was on his wife, but that he had no part in what was to happen. Here, then, we have the mystery of the "just man." Human considerations and human plans, such as those concerning marriage, must give way to God's plans, and Joseph gave way to the "mystery of Mary." But, to prevent any infringement of the rights of the legal marriage contract and to prevent Mary from being the possible subject of scandalous gossip, he decided to send her away "secretly." Joseph, the just man, was therefore motivated by religious awe.

And then came the appearance of the angel—the message to Joseph. Like the message which the angel brought to Mary, this message has an important significance within the history of salvation. Joseph was appointed, by God, to be the guardian, or foster-father, of *this* Child and the husband of *this* woman, the Mother of God: "Fear not to take unto thee Mary, thy wife." (Matt. 1. 20.) The wedding was to take place, as a result of God's word, and was to mark the consecration of their mutual cohabitation. What we have here, then, is a commission of heavenly origin which Joseph, in faith, accepted in the cause of the messianic promise of salvation. In this way, he was entrusted with a special function in the history of salvation. He became the foster-father, the paternal guardian, of the saving event here in the world. He had previously wanted to surrender his marriage rights by sending Mary away. After the angel's message, however, the meaning of his function within the history of salvation became clear. He was to marry his wife, and for him too this was to be the consecration of a *virgin* marriage.

Both for Mary and for Joseph, the Message implied a change in their already celibate lives—from that point onwards they embraced celibacy for the sake of the Kingdom of God. This celibacy was, for both of them, a personal and free commitment. The obvious initiative from which their commitment to this new, Christian celibacy had sprung was the nearness of the Child—the Messiah—who had been entrusted to them. The initiative was, however, a personal one, the outcome of their own personal decision. The angel had said nothing, either to Mary or to Joseph, about this religious decision to remain celibate in marriage. It arose directly, in both cases, from a religiosity that was in a very special way attuned to the history of Christian salvation. Mary and Joseph, therefore, supply the key to the essence of Christian celibacy— it enables the Christian to place himself at the disposal and the service of the Kingdom of Heaven.

Mary's Fiat *to the Message: Her Personal* Commitment *to Virgin Motherhood*

Mary's *fiat* was a priceless jewel of trustful faith in Yahweh. It was also the first case of explicit and free consent to the specifically *Christian* plan of redemption. Mary's gaze was directed upwards towards heaven in longing for the Messiah; God's offer, asking her if she wanted to become the mother of the Messiah, came down from heaven, and in the *fiat* this human longing and the divine offer came together. God's redeeming love and Mary's longing for redemption which embraced the longing of the whole of mankind merged into one another in Mary's positive and free response.[19] Grace had, as it were, dug its own foundations.

The *fiat* was first and foremost Mary's explicit appropriation of the Christian aspect of her own personal redemption.[20] Her free acceptance of divine motherhood as pure grace was, by definition, her own sublime "subjective redemption." She was the woman who had a Child whose name was to be "Jesus"—"Yahweh has saved." As the one who had this Child, the Redeemer, and who freely accepted this gift, Mary was the firstfruit of the Redemption. In other words, she is, *as a mother,* "sublimely redeemed." "She had a child" means that Mary had this particular Child, and the bearing of this Child, coupled with her free acceptance, in the immeasurable depth of her messianic longing, was for her both the objective gift of redemption and the appropriation of this gift, for she "conceived in faith."[21] The objective gift of her immaculate conception and the subjective holiness corresponding to her immaculate conception—her virgin state of openness—were both

---

[19] St. Bernard has imaginatively expressed the desire of the human race at the moment of the Annunciation in a passage of singular beauty. He has pictured the whole of mankind kneeling in tense anticipation of this long-awaited moment, and addressing Mary with these words: "O Lady, do not hesitate. Give the answer which heaven and earth have waited so long to hear: Delay no more and say but yes!" ("Hoc totus mundus, tuis genibus provolutus, expectabat . . . Da, Virgo, responsum festinanter. O Domina, responde verbum quod terra, quod inferi, quod expectant et superi . . . Responde itaque citius angelo, immo par angelum Domino . . . Ecce, desideratus cunctis gentibus foris pulsat ad ostium" (*Super "Missus Est,"* *Hom. IV,* 8 [*PL,* 183, col. 83–4].)

[20] It should be noted that the discussion of subjective and objective redemption in the first part of Chapter 2 deals only with *Mary's* state of being redeemed and her co-operation in her *own* redemption. In the second part of this chapter we have to consider the entire question in the light of her saving function with regard to the rest of mankind.

[21] *Fide concepit:* see St. Augustine, *Sermo Denis XXV,* 7 (Morin's ed., 162, 16–18). "Non concubuit et concepit, sed *credidit* et concepit." (*Sermo CCXXXIII,* 3, 4 [*PL,* 38, col. 1114].)

divine gifts, and prepared the way for the central, sublime event of the Annunciation within the plan of the gradual unfolding, in history, of the mystery of the Redemption. This event was in history the real gift of the Redeemer and Mary's free acceptance of this Redeemer and thus of the Redemption, since salvation, or redemption, is the very person of the incarnate God.

Mary's sublime subjective redemption thus coincided with her motherhood of the Messiah and formed one single event. She was active conception in the bodily sense and active receptivity in the spiritual sense. She allowed the Redeemer to give himself to her. All her fervent activity, her co-operation in the matter of her own redemption, was therefore on the level of receptivity—of bodily conception and spiritual reception. She was a partner in her own redemption, *ex parte recipientis*. What is accomplished in the case of every single redeemed person was accomplished, both objectively and subjectively, in a sublime manner in Mary. She was offered the gift of the Redeemer, and this gift was freely accepted. In this way she allowed the Redeemer to give himself to her, and consequently allowed redemption also to be bestowed upon her. Redemption always demands co-operation with (in faith, hope and charity), free consent to, and full acceptance of, the gift of the God-man, who, by his very calling, is the Redeemer. Mary's sublime redemption, then, is to be found in her active conception and reception of the God-man—in her perfect bodily and spiritual co-operation, her bodily and spiritual motherhood. We appropriate the objective gift of the Redeemer by our living faith, represented externally in the physical reception of the individual sacraments—*per fidem et sacramenta fidei*. Similarly, Mary was redeemed by her faith, here externally represented in her bodily reception of the primordial sacrament—the conception of Christ himself. This can be put in another way, namely that Mary was redeemed by her faithful reception, embodied in bodily conception or motherhood. She is, thus, the "Queen of Confessors."

This, then, is how the situation looks from Mary's point of view, or, to put it more precisely, from a consideration of the line of historical development of Mary's life. Her subjective state of holiness—as the sublimely redeemed person whose redemption had taken place by way of exemption—resulted in motherhood. This motherhood, viewed in the light of the gradual unfolding of events within the history of salvation, was, as it were, the organic and logical crown of her virgin receptivity and of the immeasurable depth of her longing for the Messiah. Looked at from God's point of view, on the other hand, what we have here is simply the gradual revelation of God himself, who came to redeem the world as our fellow man, as one born of our own kind, as Mary's Child.

Personal Communion with the Suffering Christ

"If sons, heirs also; heirs indeed of God and joint heirs with Christ; yet so, if we suffer with him, that we may also be glorified with him." (Rom. 8. 17.) If we are objectively redeemed by Christ's sacrificial death, then the concrete form of our subjective redemption, and thus of every single case of subjective appropriation of objective redemption, is bound to correspond to the essential meaning and direction of the objective gift. Subjective redemption is the free acceptance, the personal appropriation, of the objective gift. It is, in other words, a co-sacrifice made together with Christ. If sacrifice is regarded in this light, every redeemed human being is a co-redeemer in his own redemption. This co-redemption is, of course, not to be thought of as a contribution which adds to Christ's redemption or to our share in this redemption, as though Christ's redemption were insufficient in itself. It consists, rather, of a pure sacrificial receptivity with regard to the grace of Christ's sacrifice on the Cross. Faith, hope and charity are the channels along which this grace is received, and these three channels flow into one in sacrificial love.

Simeon's prophecy, made at the very beginning of Mary's motherhood, directed her attention to the prospect of her own suffering: "Thy own soul a sword shall pierce." (Luke 2. 35.) The third critical impulse in Mary's subjective redemption came about, once

again in a sublime manner, at the foot of the Cross. The religious
depth of her sacrificial appropriation of the Redemption brought
about by Christ alone can be understood in the light of her holiness
and the complete absence of any sin, original or actual, in her. The
significance of her co-sacrifice therefore can only be traced back to
her virgin selflessness and her immaculate generosity. As one who
was redeemed in a sublime manner, Mary was the immediate
socia passionis, the direct partner in the suffering of the Messiah,
her own flesh and blood, by way of pure reception, *participating,* in
the literal sense of the word, in the suffering of her Son by her intimate communion with the very person of Christ. Her sacrificial
love, at the foot of the Cross, was the culmination of her subjective
appropriation of the Redemption, taking the form of a redemption
through the crucified sacrificial love of the crucified Christ. She
is, therefore, the "Queen of Martyrs."

This is perhaps the best point at which to discuss Mary's physical
death. It is, of course, true that any discussion of this subject implies
a departure from the firm ground of dogmatic knowledge and an
incursion into the sphere of controversial theological opinion. Quite
a number of theologians tend, despite individual differences over
details, towards the general opinion that Mary did not in fact die
in the literal sense of the word, and claim that her body was glorified while she was still here on earth. Pope Pius XII, in his bull on
the Assumption, maintained a deliberate silence on this issue, with
the result that the Church is still not able to say with certainty
whether Mary died in the literal sense or not. The following argument, then, is put forward as a mere theological opinion, although it
forms an organic part of the entire plan of redemption and is moreover supported by very many theologians.

We have already pointed out that the dogma of the Immaculate
Conception does not in any way imply that Mary was necessarily
exempt from some of the consequences of original sin, insofar as
these were not sinful in themselves or a possible occasion for sin.
Christ himself, who was without sin, took these consequences—
suffering and death—upon himself. They constituted, in fact, the

concrete experience which Christ used to give expression and embodiment to his redemptive sacrificial love. His suffering in life and, even more particularly, his final passion and death, formed the climax of his dispossession of himself in love—*mortem moriendo destruxit*. In our case, too, physical death is the culminating point of our subjective redemption. It is the supreme expression of our sacrificial love for our Saviour and the radical separation of ourselves from sin—the ultimate death to sin. It is at the same time a perfect expiation of sin, so long as the love which inspires and animates us measures up to the objective event of death and all that death implies in terms of our dispossession of ourselves. That Mary should have died as a punishment is, of course, out of the question. But this does not mean that she did not have to die. The divine plan of subjective redemption, involving man's free consent to Christ's redemption through his death on the Cross, would appear to include Mary as well, and the implication here is that she too, as one who was redeemed (by exemption) by Christ's death, had a share in the specifically Christian death.[22] Mary, although immaculate, was nevertheless an integral *member* of the human race, which was signed with the seal of sin—that is, death—and as such she was also subject to the universal fate of mankind, although, being redeemed by exemption, death in her case was not submitted to as a punishment. But, since her exemption was the fruit of Christ's sacrificial death, it would seem that there is a close, organic connection here with the whole plan of redemption. Her

[22] This is not of course apodeictic. No "theological conclusion" in favour of the Assumption can ever be demonstrated beyond all doubt, unless it has been accepted into the living tradition of faith. This tradition of faith is, however, obscure on the subject of Mary's death, and provides no definite answer as to whether she died in the literal sense or not. It seems to me that the above argument is only acceptable so long as Mary's subjective appropriation of her own redemption is not considered in isolation, but is at the same time viewed within the context of and with special emphasis upon her co-redemptive saving function with regard to her fellow human beings. In this case the argument seems to be far more convincing. See my article "The Death of a Christian," in *Vatican II—The Struggle of Minds, and Other Essays,* Dublin, M. H. Gill and Son (1963), pp. 61–91.

utter dedication to God and her dispossession of herself were, there-fore, perfectly expressed and embodied in her physical death. Mary's death—her *dormitio,* or "falling asleep in love"—can thus be seen as the supreme example of every Christian death, and contained the promise of immediate resurrection. This took place at once in Mary's case. Her assumption, on death, became an im-mediate reality.

Mary's Pentecost

This last mystery of Christ was accomplished after his ascen-sion. The Acts describe how the Apostles were "persevering with one mind in prayer, with . . . Mary, the mother of Jesus" (Acts 1. 14). Before the Annunciation, Mary's life formed the culminating point and the synthesis of the entire Old Testament longing for the Messiah. In the Cenacle, after Christ's ascension, Mary can be seen as synthesizing, in her life, the longing for the spirit of Christ. Faithful to the basic interior law of her immaculate being, still the essence of active receptivity, she continued to play exactly the same part in the drama. The descent of the Holy Ghost was, for her, the beginning of the last stage in the mystery of her spiritual life. Her religious appropriation of Christ's redemption was deepened by the Pentecostal experience and her understanding, through faith, of the entire plan of salvation was increased. The experience of Pentecost meant at the same time that her universal significance within the plan of salvation (this subject will have to be discussed in greater detail at a later stage) became for her too an event of explicit awareness and freely accepted activity. In faith she attained at Pen-tecost the summit of her understanding of her true place at the very heart and centre of the young Church.

What emerges from the foregoing is, then, that the Mother of God was both objectively and subjectively a redeemed person, re-deemed in an exceptional and unique manner, and that it was her spiritual and bodily motherhood which formed the central core of her objective and subjective redemption. At the same time, however, it can be seen that her partnership in her own redemption was also the result of her being fundamentally the "sublimely redeemed."

God Accepts Mary's Life-Offering: Her Assumption into Heaven

The essential moment of Christ's act of redemption is not restricted to his sacrificial death. The divine acceptance of the sacrifice is complementary and co-essential to that sacrifice. This acceptance by God is in fact Jesus' *resurrection*. The absolute sacrifice of atonement, through which the human race was reunited to God in love, is to be found in Christ's passion—his transition from death to life. Both Christ's death and his resurrection therefore constitute the two mysteries of the Redemption, and these form a single, indivisible whole. The Resurrection is Christ's sacrifice accepted by God, and it was only at the Resurrection that the sacrifice became fully effective. At that moment, "objective redemption" became a perfect reality.

Going a stage further, we can, by analogy with Christ's resurrection, conclude from the fact of Mary's *resurrection* that her life-sacrifice was also fully accepted by God. Her assumption into heaven was not merely a privilege bestowed on her without relation to the rest of her life. It formed the summit of her sublime redemption. Salvation, after all, embraces the *whole* human being, not only his soul but also his body. The permanent spiritual and physical togetherness of the human being with Christ glorified and, in Christ, with the Trinity, forms the final and unceasing phase of the redemptive process. With this phase, redemption is completed. Dogma informs us that Mary was not obliged to wait, as we are, until the end of time for physical redemption. This is a clear indication of the unique quality of her sublime state of redemption. It also illuminates the fact of her redemption by exemption—that at no moment of her existence did sin cast a shadow over the brightness of her life with God. However blessed they may be in heaven, the other saints are, in a manner of speaking, still in a state of expectation. What must surely emerge from this is a realization of the unspeakable enormity of the destructive effect of *mankind's* sin, which, so to speak, still continues to make itself felt in those saints who have not yet been glorified. At the same time, however, we can, by contrast, comprehend the full holiness of God's majesty. This very state of blessedness in heaven, which the saints enjoy only *in their souls,* throws light upon the unassailable quality of God's holiness. It indicates quite clearly the share which the body has in the glory of heaven, as an essential element of the full Christian salvation. The fact of Mary's assumption into heaven, which is already accomplished, is illustrative of her sublime and perfect subjective redemption.

MARY'S UNIVERSAL PARTNERSHIP IN OUR SUBJECTIVE REDEMPTION

Since redemption always implies reception and co-operation on the part of man, and in view of the fact that Mary co-operated in the most profound way in the work of her own redemption, she is therefore, in this respect, the prototype of all those who receive redemption, thus of all who are redeemed. In this way she possesses a universal significance for all of us within the plan of salvation. She is the prototype of the redeemed life, the full and ultimate realization of every Christian life. Mary, the *Assumpta,* stands before us as the firstfruit of the Redemption, and incorporates the perfect features of everything that has to be realized in us and in the whole Church.

We are at once faced with a problem here. "Objective redemption," as we have already observed, implies that what has still to take place in us has already been fully realized in Christ. But now we have reached the point where we must recognize that Mary's subjective state of redemption is of a special kind. "Subjective redemption" was brought about in her in a perfect and sublime manner, with the result that she too gained a "typical" value with regard to all of us, in our life of redemption. This situation, then,

makes it necessary for us to consider at a deeper level the relationship between Mary's subjective redemption and the "objective
redemption" which has already been accomplished in Christ.

Whatever the outcome of this closer examination of the subject may be, the foregoing has definitely established one point very
firmly. All Mary's activity within the plan of salvation must of
necessity be redeemed activity, an intimate activity consisting
of pure reception and conception with regard to Christ. For if we,
along with the entire religious tradition which is common to both
the East and the West, are bound to acknowledge that Mary's acts
of faith have a universal saving value for all men, then we are
obviously able to look for this only within the special, that is, the
unique and exceptional, place which Mary occupies among *redeemed* human beings. We have already seen that there was no
single moment during her life at which she was, as it were, not
implicated in the Redemption, which was brought by Christ alone
and freely accepted by her. It is therefore not enough for us to
attribute this redemption to Mary and simply to add that this came
about in subordination to Christ. An assertion of this kind would
have the immediate effect of diminishing the unique quality of
Christ's redemptive mediation. It would be quite wrong, even if the
proviso were made that Mary was subordinate to Jesus in the
matter of redemption, to regard them both as *unredeemed* principles of the Redemption. It is impossible to separate Mary from
her state of redemption. Even if we were to place her next to and
subordinate to Christ, in opposition to the whole of humanity—
and this may appear to be the case at a later stage of this book—
she would nonetheless continue to occupy this place as the sublimely redeemed. The tension would, however, still remain between Mary's position as a member of redeemed mankind and her
universally predominant position among the whole of the human
race. The unity which exists between these two basic truths may
give us a sound understanding of the character of Mary's universal
role within the plan of salvation. Her universal receptivity with
regard to Christ may be said to rest on the foundation of her uni-

versal gift with regard to us. To express this idea in a different way, her universal saving function with regard to us can be considered as an aspect of the sublime and unique nature of her *state* of being redeemed, her spiritual and bodily receptivity, that is, her reception and conception. Although this undoubtedly characterizes her entire existence, it reaches its peak at certain definite moments in her life. It is at these culminating points too that her function as our co-redemptrix gains its highest expression. What we may conclude from this, then, is how closely Mary's function in the matter of our salvation is bound up with the moments of particular grace due to *her* state of being both objectively and subjectively redeemed.

Mary, Universal Prototype of Christians and Our Active Model

As we have already said, Mary, like us, had also to accept her own redemption freely. In this way, she became a "co-redemptrix" in her own redemption. We can, however, go a stage further than this. Her co-operation in receiving redemption possessed a theological depth which corresponded to the sublime and exceptional manner in which the Redeemer, and thus redemption, was bestowed upon her. As a consequence of this, her co-operation in her own redemption was incomparably greater than our co-operation in our redemption. We can therefore reasonably claim that Mary is our prototype and model, and that we may, in faith, confidently acknowledge her as such, in our positive response to the Redemption which is brought to us by the God-man, Christ, alone. In this respect, then, Mary stands as the pattern of the Christian attitude towards life, and every Christian should look upon her as his constant example. This universal ideal and this exemplary quality of Mary's holiness is, therefore, *one* aspect of her function in the plan of salvation.

This particular function is, of course, of the same order as the exemplary role which all the saints play in our own life of grace.

But even at this level, a comparison can only be made between Mary and the other saints provided that we recognize Mary's immeasurably higher status and the unique place which she occupies in the Christian order of the communion of saints. This initial distinction, although it is quite radical, is, of course, only a relative one, as it were, in the depth of God-centred life. It is, however, fundamental to the divine plan.

It is possible to go even deeper into this question, and to consider something which gives Mary an *absolute* uniqueness which raises her above the level of all such merely relative distinctions and which applies to her alone and to no other saint. It is this element which has been responsible for the exceptional cult of Mary in the life of the Church—a veneration which comes second only to that of Christ himself. This deeper aspect of the Marian mystery is also the key to the basic difference between the Catholic and the Protestant attitudes towards Mary—a sure indication that it lies at the very heart of the Christian concept of the Redemption.

Mary's Virgin Motherhood of Men: the Deeper Meaning of Her Fiat

Through her *fiat* Mary allowed the Redeemer to bestow himself upon her. The sublime manner of her own redemption was apparent from the fact that she was redeemed in an unfathomable faith, externalized in the bodily conception of the gift of the primordial sacrament, the God-man himself, Jesus Christ.

There is, however, even more to Mary's sublimity. This is to be found in the unique quality of the *object* of her positive assent, to which the exceptional depth of her *fiat* fully corresponded.

The Mother of Christ, Head of all mankind.—Mary, of whom Christ was born as the true child of Adam (Luke 3. 38; cf. 23–38), is thus the link by which Christ's holy and redeeming humanity is bound to our humanity. Thanks to Mary's positive assent to the Message, God was, as man, genuinely *ex hominibus assumptus, ex stirpe Adam*—of our generation of Adam, that is to say, *a true man*.

In the *concrete* sense, the Incarnation is the Redemption in principle, since Christ is, by definition, incarnate God. The concrete significance and purpose of the Incarnation is, according to God's intention, redemption by a man who was called to this task by a divine vocation, to be the representative of the whole of human kind. As we have already said, Christ is, by his vocation, the representative of the entire human community. The divine incarnation is, in the concrete sense, a religious and supernatural event, the offer to all men of divine life in Christ, the real Son of God. This offer applies to all men. The reason for this is that Christ is, by vocation, the head of the entire human race, and, further, that he reveals, in his concrete human appearance, the vocation of the entire human race. This offer must be, and indeed is, a real one, by virtue of the fact of God becoming our fellow-man. God's incarnation, then, implies, in the concrete sense, a real, spiritual and supernatural vocation which is directed by God towards all men. The reality of this vocation is not to be found in any extrinsic "divine decree." On the contrary, the concrete appearance of the God-man himself—God himself as an offer to all his fellow men in the man Jesus Christ—constitutes this reality. The fundamental principle, on which all the teaching of the Fathers and the medieval Schoolmen concerning Christ was based, is that God became man so that man might be deified.

From this it follows that Mary, in her *fiat* to the Message, gave her free consent to become the mother of Christ, the representative of the whole of mankind. This formed the basis of her freely accepted spiritual motherhood with regard to all men. She became the mother of the vocation of all men, the mother of the vocation revealed to us in the incarnate God. The unity of the whole of the human race can exist essentially only in a unity established in a community of persons, all of whom are filled with one and the same vocation. The single, unifying vocation common to all members of this community, which was given to all men in Adam and was consequently lost by him, was renewed historically in a sublime manner in the God-man Christ, and re-established at a far deeper level.

As the mother of Christ, who embodies, tangibly and visibly, this vocation of all men, Mary is also the mother of this personal community of human beings in the realization of their life-destiny. Thus we are able to claim that, because of the essential significance of her concrete motherhood, Mary is already fundamentally the mother of all the redeemed.

The meaning of Mary's virgin state in her motherhood with regard to all men.—This view of Mary's motherhood can also show us her virginity in a new perspective and disclose its deeper significance. What, then, is this new meaning which Mary's virgin state gained after the Message? It is that she became a virgin *in* motherhood, that hers was a virgin motherhood. She was not a virgin and yet, at the same time, also a mother. She was a mother and virgin, a virgin-mother. She prolonged the heavenly gift of her virgin motherhood into a state of celibacy which she freely took upon herself. Her single purpose, as a mother, was to belong exclusively to the Redeemer. Her virgin state, embraced "for the sake of the Kingdom of God," gave her motherhood an apostolic significance. When she conceived Christ in her womb this was not an act of procreation, as the outcome of love between a husband and wife, the mark and seal upon their mutual affection for each other. It follows, then, that her conception of Christ in no way implied a "possession" of her Child, as a mother "possesses" or "owns" the child she has conceived as the result of the mutual love existing between her and her husband. On the contrary, it implies that she conceived Christ and became the mother of the Messiah for the benefit of the whole of mankind—"for the sake of the Kingdom of God."[23] In her becoming the mother of a child, then, she belonged absolutely and as a virgin to God. Her virgin motherhood is therefore essentially a religious and apostolic event. The virgin

[23] This view of the virgin state of Mary's motherhood seems to me to be more convincing than the view taken by many other theologians. It is impossible to avoid the impression, in connection with many of these other opinions, that married relationships, even in the case of partners of exceptional holiness, are to some extent, however slightly, regarded as "somehow not quite all right."

state of her divine motherhood, viewed as an aspect of this motherhood, serves to emphasize the fact that she became the mother of
Christ precisely for the benefit of all men.

What is striking in this context is that Mary's subjective redemption was already beginning, at this point, to display signs of her
direct co-operation in Christ's active redemption for our benefit.
She conceived the Redeemer as her own Child, for the benefit of
all men. The first part of this sentence—Mary's conception of
"Christ, the Redeemer, as her own Child"—clearly indicates the
sublimity both of the objective gift of redemption which she received and of her subjective co-operation in her own redemption
(see the preceding section of this chapter). The second half of the
sentence—Mary's conception of Christ "for the benefit of all men"
—points to the apostolic, saving function with regard to us which
her sublime state of redemption, both objective and subjective, implied.

In was not in the least necessary for Mary to be explicitly aware
of all these implications in order that, from the very outset, her
motherhood with regard to us should be a conscious acceptance of
or a free personal commitment to this special function within the
plan of salvation. Certainly she knew, with explicit awareness, that
her Child was to be the Messiah, the Redeemer of Israel and of
mankind. This knowledge was sufficient for her to commit herself
to her task, which was, at the same time, apostolic.

*Mary's personal communion with Christ in the historical event of
redemption.*—Both the views which we have just outlined can be
seen in their full dimensions if we take a closer look at the *unique*
quality of the object of Mary's positive assent to the Redemption
at the time of the Message, as opposed to the object of our assent
to the redemption brought by Christ. This object is the historical
event of the Redemption, to be objectively accomplished in Christ.
By virtue of the redemption which was to come, and thus by grace,
Mary's *fiat* to the Message actually conditioned objective redemption in its sacramental and historical fulfilment, at the level
of the historical unfolding of the plan of salvation. The unique

quality of this object of Mary's subjective redemption thus contains the implication that her *fiat* simultaneously provided the objective potentiality of the salvation of all mankind. Mary, therefore, is not of the same order or status as her co-redeemed fellow men and fellow believers. In the sentence which was the subject of our consideration in the foregoing section Mary's act of faith emerged, not simply as an element which played a contributory part in the dispensation of redemptive grace, but as a critical moment which formed a constitutional part of Christ's objective redemption. At the Annunciation Mary gave her conscious consent to the Messiah, the Saviour of the People, thus accepting, in faith and physically, the accomplishment of the objective event of the Redemption, for the benefit of all men, and consequently conditioning this event at the historical level. She therefore became a partner in the redemption brought by Christ himself.

It should, however, be constantly borne in mind that Mary's direct co-operation in God's concrete redemptive incarnation rested firmly on the basis of her active conception and reception. Her personal, holy acceptance of motherhood was a prior effect of the merits of Christ's human actions. It was in this way that the God-man, Jesus Christ, penetrated into the very core of the concrete motherhood to which Mary had been called by God alone. Her meritoriousness cannot in any way be dissociated from the overriding merits of Christ himself. Thus, at the level of the Redemption in its historically concrete sense, Mary never emerges as a second principle of the Redemption, and is never parallel, in this sense, with Christ.

It is, however, apparent that her active conception and reception of the Redeemer implied not only co-operation with regard to her own sublime "subjective redemption" but also co-operation in Christ's objective redemption for the benefit of mankind. This latter co-operation was equally a result of her spiritual and bodily conception and reception of Christ. Mary's *fiat* to the Message which announced the Incarnation and thus the Redemption was a conscious, free appropriation of her own *Christian* redemption and at the same time formed a constitutional element of the historical redemption of the whole of mankind which was accomplished in Christ.

We have already frequently referred to the sublime manner of Mary's redemption, and by "redemption" we have meant her subjective redemption both with respect to the objective gift of grace and with respect to her free, personal appropriation of this gift. It should now be possible to see the sublimity of Mary's redemption in this sense in its true and full dimensions—to see Mary, in other words, as the receiving and co-operating principle of our redemption. By this we mean, in the first place, that Mary was, in her active conception and receptivity, the co-operating principle in "objective redemption," in that she was personally involved in the objective reality of *our* redemption in the man Jesus, and shared in the objective fact of the state of redemption of the whole of mankind brought about in principle in *Christ*. This idea can also be expressed in this way—mankind was, in a real sense, reconciled with the Father, both in Christ as Redeemer and in Mary as the firstfruit of the redemption, the first of the redeemed. In the second place, what is meant by Mary as the receiving and co-operating principle of our redemption is that she was the receiving and co-operating principle in our subjective redemption, both in its aspect as an objective gift and in our meritorious personal appropriation of the gift.

Her spiritual reception and bodily conception of Christ can thus be seen as a gift for us. In allowing the Redeemer to bestow himself upon her, in her pure conception of the Son of God, she gave us the only Mediator, Jesus Christ, who was grace itself. At the same time she allowed the Redeemer to bestow himself on *her* and on the whole of mankind, and thus became—still on the level of receptive co-operation—"obediens, et sibi et universi generi humano causa facta est salutis,"[24] a partner in the redeeming mystery of Christ and a collaborator in our redemption, and precisely in and through her sublime personal appropriation of her *own* sublime redemption. The superabundance of what she obtained

[24] St. Irenaeus, *Adversus Haereses*, 3, 22, 4 (*PG*, 7, col. 959).

from Christ was the cause in her of the superabundance of her merits. In faith she conceived Christ, God made man in her womb, the primordial sacrament and the sole origin of salvation. For her, "having a child" meant giving a divine Child to the world. For that reason, she is not only the universally redeemed, the prototype of the whole of redeemed mankind and of the Church. She is also, by reason of her freely accepted motherhood with regard to Christ, who is, by his vocation, the head of the whole of mankind, fundamentally the mother of the whole of redeemed mankind. She is, moreover, not only the mother of all Christians, but also the mother of all those who are not yet members of the Christian Church. She is the mother of every apostolate and every mission. She is the mother of all men because she was a partner in the objective work of redemption which applies to all men.

It is important and indeed necessary to affirm Mary's direct part in the objective redemption and at the same time to insist that, this direct role presupposed, we can avoid an inner conflict between the statements that Mary was herself redeemed and that she has this function, only if Mary's part in objective redemption was a *co-operation based on pure receptivity;* and if this receptivity, because of the unique quality of its object (to which Mary's *fiat,* with its exceptional and profound implications, fully corresponded) was also an exceptional and universal "conception" or reception, extending in its total influence to all men.

Mary's Personal Communion with Christ in His Self-Offering on the Cross

A possible objection to the foregoing which we are bound to consider is that a direct role in God's incarnation, although based on pure receptivity and having a universal influence, does not necessarily imply a role in Christ's redemptive death and that, for this reason, it is not possible to regard Mary as the mother of the mystical body, which was brought into being through Christ's sacrificial death, except in a very remote sense. This assertion is, in my opinion, not justified, for the following reasons.

Mary's consent, in faith, to the Message as an implicit acceptance of the sacrifice of the Cross.—Looked at in its concrete reality, God's incarnation is essentially redemptive. No other real divine incarnation is known to us. Mary became the mother of the Messiah, the *Ebed Yahweh,* the servant of God whose coming was foretold in Scripture. The whole of Christ's life was essentially a reparation of human sinfulness, a redemption, and his death on the Cross formed the climax to which his divine and human life of redemption was inwardly directed from its earliest beginning. His sacrificial death was present, in an embryonic form, at the very first moment of his existence. This ultimate goal was formulated in more precise terms and its implications made clearer by Christ himself, in his frequent references to his "hour," but only towards the end of his life. Mary had no conscious knowledge of it at the time of the Message, nor had she any need of such knowledge. In faith, she freely accepted the Messiah, the Redeemer, and this explicit acceptance included all the conditions which God might subsequently impose on the life of the Messiah. What those conditions were, Mary was to learn, step by step, throughout the course of her Child's life. Her positive answer to the Message, made in faith, meant that she was ready to surrender herself, in faith, to whatever might happen, to the incalculable element, to all the ultimate possibilities of the divine plan. From the objective point of view, this incalculable element was the Crucifixion. The virgin depth of her faithful assent to the Message, however, enabled Mary, subjectively, to remain completely open to every divine possibility. This constituted her implicit consent to the Crucifixion. Her explicit acceptance of the Redeemer of the world, for our benefit, constituted at the same time her implicit, free consent to the suffering which the Messiah was to undergo for our sake. This basic openness, present in her acceptance of the offer of motherhood with regard to Christ, and of her consequent motherhood with regard to all men, which was basically implied in her motherhood of Christ (see pp. 81 ff.), means that she too was directed inwardly towards a later, explicit consent to the sacrifice of the Cross. Mary was, therefore, in a *fundamental* sense, the spiritual mother of the human race as redeemed *by the Cross* even at the time of the Annunciation.

Mary's explicit communion with Christ in his self-offering on the Cross.—We must now turn to a consideration of Mary's communion in Christ's sacrifice at the foot of the Cross. Because of her immaculate state, her suffering was clearly not due to a punishment for personal sinfulness. It represented rather an integral experience, an embodiment of her subjective redemption in the specifically Christian sense. This view can disclose the deeper implications of Mary's role during the Crucifixion. Her communion with Christ's suffering made her initial "Be it done unto me according to thy word" fully explicit. The object of her martyrdom was the martyrdom of the Redeemer himself. As a mother, her suffering was Christ's suffering. Her communion with Christ was, therefore, determined by Christ's sacrifice at the historical moment of its accomplishment. In this sense she, and she alone, was directly involved in Christ's redemptive act.

With sacrificial love she expressly consented to and acquiesced in Christ's passion and death. The sacrificial aspect of her subjective appropriation of the grace of redemption won by the Crucifixion thereby gained full and conscious expression. Her sacrificial love in this respect is at the same time the explicit continuation of her initial bodily conception and spiritual reception of the Redeemer for the benefit of all men. In sacrifice and in suffering with Christ she explicitly accepted at this point the redemption of the Cross, and did this for the sake of all men, since this active acceptance formed the explication of her earlier act of conception and reception of Christ. In the fullest sense she was the mother both of Christ crucified and of the Mystical Body which was brought into being by the Crucifixion. This is why Pope Pius XII was able to say, in his encyclical *Mystici Corporis,* that Mary's communion in Christ's suffering at the foot of the Cross gave her a "renewed claim" to motherhood with regard to us, a new title derived from the explicit continuation of her completely open *fiat* to the vital, living implication contained in the Message, of which she, in her initial acceptance of the total mystery, was not aware in all its concrete future potentiality. Her conception and reception of the God-man Christ formed the deeper basis of this intensified motherhood. We, as Christians, are all born of this mutual sacrificial and suffering love of Jesus and his mother. Thus, what began as Mary's consent to virgin motherhood of the Redeemer, who was the representative of the entire human race, was accomplished here in sacrificial love.

Mary's "Constitution in Power"—the Glorification of the Mother of Men

"Christ Jesus, who, being in the form of God, thought it not robbery to be equal with God, but emptied himself, taking the form of a servant, being made in the likeness of men, and in habit found as a man. He humbled himself, becoming obedient unto death, even to the death of the cross. For which cause, God also hath exalted him and hath given him a name which is above all names . . . that every tongue should confess that Jesus Christ is the Lord." (Phil. 2. 5–11.) The dignity and power of the Redeemer as Lord—his "coming into power" as St. Paul calls it (Rom. 1. 4)—are the most profound element of the paschal mystery of Easter: his resurrection, his ascension and his "sitting at the right hand of the Father," i.e., the triumphant entry into God's sovereign prerogative. Although Christ was the Messiah from birth, his saving function, as the Messiah, was a reality which grew in him. His messianic death enabled him to reach the summit of his messiahship in the Resurrection, and it was the resurrection which made him "Kyrios."

What is striking in this context is that Jesus was, during that phase of his existence which we may call his *kenosis,* in other words, during his earthly life, working, so to speak, at "half strength." For years he instructed and educated his Apostles. They, however, show every sign of not having understood him, right up to the time of his death. But, from the moment that Christ received the full measure of the Holy Spirit on his resurrection—as soon as he was "constituted in power"—the Apostles were, so to speak, changed at a single stroke in virtue of his sending the Spirit. About three thousand people were baptized, according to the Acts of the Apostles, after Peter's first sermon. (Acts 2. 41.) "Being exalted therefore by the right hand of God, and having received of the Father the promise of the Holy Ghost, he hath poured forth this [over us]." (Acts 2. 33.) Christ was made, by his resurrection, into a "quickening spirit." (1 Cor. 15. 45; see also 2 Cor. 3. 17.) And St. John gives us the fruit of his meditations in this phrase: "And I, if I be lifted up from the earth, will draw all things to myself." (John 12. 32.)

It is thus clear from scriptural evidence that the full measure of Christ's messianic power came to him with his resurrection. Christ "in the days of his flesh . . . learned obedience by the things that he suffered. And, being consummated [i.e., glorified], he became, to all that obey him, the cause of eternal salvation." (Heb. 5. 7–9.) The full power and efficacy of his sacrifice of atonement came with the Resurrection.

Mary, as the maternal partner in Christ's redemptive activity, shared in his power as Lord by virtue of her assumption into heaven. Her resurrection is the "constitution in power" of her motherhood with regard to all men. Her intercession on our behalf in heaven cannot be conceived as a pale reflection of her share in the Redemption here on earth. Mary, in heaven, is our mother "in power," just as Jesus, in heaven, is the "Son of God in power." (Rom. 1. 4.) The Virgin Mary's queenship is the ultimate fruit, the crowning, both of her state of redemption and of her role in the Redemption. It represents her share in her Son's "sitting at the right hand of the Father," the Son who was both her Redeemer and ours. The introduction of the new liturgical feast of Mary's queenship by Pope Pius XII was a direct outcome of the dogma of the Assumption and at the same time an implicit affirmation of Mary's function in the Redemption.

Her glorification, or "constitution in power," is also an enthronement as mother. Her heavenly power is still confined essentially to her maternal function and is effective within the mysterious relationship existing between the glorified Mother and the *Kyrios,* her Son, Jesus, in whose name "every knee should bow, of those that are in heaven, on earth, and under the earth" (Phil. 2. 10).

For Mary, this is pure grace and election. It is, however, also God's recognition of her commitment to faith on earth as a mother and the divine reward for her sacrificial life. In heaven, Mary continues in a glorified manner the maternal task which she began on earth.

CONCLUSION: MARY'S COMMUNION WITH CHRIST IN HIS SAVING WORK ON EARTH AND HIS DISPENSING OF GRACE IN HEAVEN

The foregoing analysis is bound to lead the believer to the positive affirmation that the Mother of God's role in the objective redemption, conferred upon the world by the God-man Christ alone, was direct, purely receptive and thus universal in its influence. He is bound to recognize further that there was a consequent co-operation on Mary's part in our subjective redemption, which is, after all, no more or less than the ultimate goal, the mature fruit, of our objective redemption. It is only with reference to a universal co-operation on Mary's part, by means of pure receptivity, that we are able, and indeed obliged, to assert that Mary co-operated directly in the Redemption, since a co-operation of this kind does indeed possess a real and essential value of its own and is inherently efficacious, but it is not efficacious in addition to the redeeming activity of Christ, the only Mediator. Mary was the universally receptive, the universally redeemed, and *in this way* she shares in our redemption. It is, moreover, only by viewing her function in this light that it is possible to avoid arriving at a false conclusion from the principle "principium meriti non cadit sub merito," namely, that Mary, because she was herself fully redeemed, cannot possibly be a co-principle in the Redemption. Only if we stress that Mary's co-operation was purely receptive, and understand this co-operation as her communion with the redeeming Christ, the sole Redeemer, can we avoid the interpretation that any form of co-operation on Mary's part in the Redemption is absurd.

We must, however, bear in mind that the divine redemption of mankind is still a redemption which has to be *freely accepted* by man and is thus a humanly meritorious redemption. To put this in another way, we should constantly keep in mind that there must be personal acceptance of redemption. If we do this, it at once becomes clear that it was precisely Mary's objective and subjective state of being redeemed which formed the basis both of her universal activity and her universal merits with regard to her own redemption and ours, both in the objective and subjective sense. This was so by virtue of her spiritual and bodily motherhood, to which she freely committed herself in faith, or, in other words, by virtue of the sublime manner in which she was both objectively and subjectively redeemed because of the unique quality of the object[25] of her free acceptance which, in its turn, comprised a correspondingly unique depth of faith and readiness for sacrifice. The solution is to be found in Mary's pure spiritual and therefore active receptivity. This sacrificial receptivity also points the way to an understanding of the special property of her universal activity, which is in itself one of the fruits, and indeed of the most important fruits, of the redemption which was brought by the God-man to all men.

It follows, then, that there can be no question of regarding Mary's part in the Redemption as a contribution made together with Christ and in addition to Christ's redeeming act, so as to make up for whatever might be lacking in Christ's "sufficient" redemption. On the contrary, the conclusion which we must draw is that the universally receptive Mother of God—the universal *fiat* —received everything from Christ for the benefit of all men. Because she possessed this receptive capacity and acted within it, and because the object of her *fiat* was unique, she was also able to pass everything which she received on to all men. For this

[25] That is, divine motherhood, having Christ—Redemption—as her own Child.

reason, the Christian community owes everything both to Christ and to his mother, though at totally different levels. The reality and the irreplaceable value of Mary's own activity is in no way nullified by this universal saving efficacy based on pure receptivity, since, even if this receptivity is derived from God, as a gift of grace, neither God nor the God-man can ever perform our personal act for us. I always remain the subject of my own individual action, and this basic law applies equally to Mary and her free, personal act—the act which enabled God to enter the world and fulfil his vocation within the Christian plan of salvation. Mary's act, then, was an essential element in both objective and subjective redemption.

Mary is therefore the "mother of grace," the mother of the God-man Christ, who alone possesses the absolute fullness of grace which was drawn upon by Mary and is drawn upon by all members of the Mystical Body, quite independently of her. The various statements concerning our redemption by Christ as the new Adam together with Mary as the new Eve are borne out in the whole of the traditional teaching of the Church, though only on condition that Mary's co-operation be regarded as active spiritual and physical receptivity, and not as an additional principle in some way making up for a deficiency in Christ's redemption. This seems to me to have a very important practical bearing upon our present-day preaching on the subject of Mary and our attempts to guide devotion to Mary in a truly Christian direction. The universal mediation of Christ's mother and ours is not a mediation of a head in relation to the members, but a mediation of a member among members—of a member who is, by virtue of the objectively and subjectively sublime manner of her own redeemed state, an exceptional and unique member of the Mystical Body.[26] In this respect, that is to say, as the mother of the whole Christian community, Mary is placed high above the Mystical Body. (It should be noted in this context that Mary is traditionally often

[26] See St. Augustine, *Sermo XXV de Verbis Evang. Matt. XII,* 4–50 (*PL,* 46, col. 938).

referred to as the "neck" which joins the members of the body to its head.) Her state of being redeemed, which comprises a universal saving function with regard to all the co-redeemed, makes Mary the active prototype of the "communion of saints" redeemed by Christ. She is the universally conceptive, life-bearing womb of the Christian community, the type of the Church. Her mother-hood, spiritual and bodily, in faith, the motherhood to which she freely committed herself in faith, forms the synthesis of Mary's objectively and subjectively sublime redemption. Her specific in-fluence and mediation of grace with regard to us are also included in her motherhood.

It is therefore impossible for us to reconcile this view with the views of certain theologians who tend to place Mary on a com-pletely different basis within the plan of salvation and seek to make her God's partner in the work of salvation. Their reasoning is based on the premise that, though Christ is truly man, he is not a human person. Atonement essentially implies a reconciliation between distinct and separate *persons,* and in the case of the Redemption, this means a reconciliation between God as the party who effects the reconciliation and the human race as the party to be reconciled. In addition to the divine subject, and in the real sense quite distinct from this subject, it was, in the case of the Redemption, necessary to find a human subject able, as a human person, to represent the human race as a whole. In view of the fact that Christ is not, according to the principle upon which the argument of these theologians is based, a human person, then it is obvious that Mary had to be this person.

In my opinion, any Marian doctrine based upon a principle such as this is bound to result in a deep misunderstanding of the Incarnation and of the unique mediation of Christ. As St. Paul says, "there is one God, and one mediator of God and men, the man Christ Jesus, who gave himself as a ransom for all, a testimony in due times."[27] It is a dogma of the Church that the God-man

[27] 1 Tim. 2. 5–6. St. Paul is not thinking of Mary here, but of the many different heavenly beings whom the gnostics of his own time regarded as

is one person, not two persons, and if theologians have constantly affirmed that there is no human person in Christ, the Church has never understood this in the sense of a lack or deficiency in Christ's true humanity. *Personally* the second person of the Trinity is truly man. Since the God-man was himself a person, he perfectly incorporated in himself all that was necessary for the reconciliation of God and men. He himself *is* this reconciliation. Otherwise Mary would be in the strictest sense of the word the co-redemptrix, as a principle in addition to Christ, though subordinate to him. In this case Mariology would be totally different. Mary would no longer be seen to function as essential receptivity, as the traditional teaching of the Church has always maintained. Viewed in this way, she would take over those essential saving functions which in fact belong to Christ's humanity. The humanity of Christ would then merge imperceptibly into his divinity. As a result of this, it is highly probable that the half-conscious notion that Mary, the human being, brings Christ, the God, closer to us would become prevalent in popular devotion to Mary. A false devotion of this kind to Mary would inevitably have the most harmful effects on the sacramental life of the Christian community, since it is by the sacraments that we are directly joined to Christ's humanity, and thus to God.

In refuting this view, it is necessary to stress the fact that it was Jesus himself who first spoke the *fiat* to the Redemption, in the name of all men. It is Christ alone, not Mary, who is our representative with the Father. The man Jesus is not only the concrete and visible realization of the *divine offer of love* which God made to men. He is also the absolute and pure realization of the

---

mediators between God and men. The Church has, however, always fully understood the unique mediation of Christ, to which St. Paul refers in this passage. No attempt has ever been made, in the traditional teaching of the Church, to minimize Christ's unique function as Mediator by, for example, a false appeal to the fact that St. Paul did not mark the end of public revelation, and that St. John, in his later writings, which deal in a more explicit way with Mary's place in the plan of salvation, considerably toned down what St. Paul had said in this and similar passages.

human response of love made to this offer on God's part. It is as if God himself departed from his divine viewpoint and entered creation as a man in order to make this response himself to his invitation to love, by means of a personal living experience of the conditions of our human existence, exclusive of sin. God, the free person who invites us to love, is in his humanity at the same time the free person who accepts this love in the name of us all. It would be a grave error to deprive Christ of this profound reality in order to ascribe it to Mary. In so doing, we should be guilty of a complete failure to grasp the deepest implications of the Incarnation, for this can never be regarded simply as an event brought about by God in the man Christ. In Jesus, the God-man, the Incarnation was also a spiritual "consent" in the name of us all— in accordance with the conditions imposed by Christ's true humanity. In the Epistle to the Hebrews Jesus' conscious human life is summarized thus: ". . . behold, I come . . . to do thy will, O God" (Heb. 10.7).

Christ himself, in our name, pronounced the *fiat* to the Redemption. Mary's *fiat*—her assent in faith—on the other hand, was her free consent to the work of redemption which was freely accepted by the God-man Christ, and this *fiat*, or assent in faith, has a universally meritorious value in respect of the *fiat* which every believer has to make. It is for this reason that St. Thomas declared that "the *fiat* made by the Blessed Virgin, the *fiat* which was expected of her in the Message, was her personal act and hers alone, but it had its repercussion on the salvation of many in the world, and indeed on the salvation of the whole of the human race."[28] The Collect of the Feast of Our Lady Mediatrix of All Graces, cele-

[28] "Consensus Beatae Virginis qui per annuntiationem requirebatur, actus singularis personae erat, in multitudinis salutem redundans, immo totius humani generis" (*III Sent.*, d. 3, q. 3, a. 2, sol. 2, pp. 125–6 in the Moos edition), and in this sense, the *consensus* is to be understood as a "consensus Virginis loco totius humanae naturae." (*ST, III,* q. 30, a. 1.) In other words, Mary gave her consent as mother, with the result that this consent has a universal significance for all men. This is different, however, from the consent of the man Jesus, who was the representative of the whole of humanity.

brated on 8 May, illustrates this doctrine beautifully: "Lord Jesus Christ, our mediator with the Father, who have deigned to constitute the blessed Virgin Mary, your mother, our mother too and our mediatrix with you, grant in your kindness that whoever approaches you seeking favours should rejoice to have obtained all things through her."[29]

What this Collect states explicitly is that Christ is the mediator between God, the Father, and *men*, and that Mary is the mediatrix between Christ and us. This in no way implies that our experience of Christ is not *direct* and without intervention, but that everything that we have to ask of Christ and all our co-operation with his redemptive grace is intimately connected with the real vocational priority of Mary's *fiat* and her acceptance of the Redeemer who is our grace. Mary became our mother by reason of her vocation, a vocation which was ontologically based in, and became visible in, her motherhood of the God-man, the head of mankind. This vocation was freely accepted by Mary in her *fiat,* both to the Message and to the sacrifice of the Cross. In other words, hers was a committed motherhood, which in turn implies a maternal relationship with all her children and an abiding motherly solicitude for them. The objective bond which exists between Mary's motherhood and our lives as Christians, even before we become aware of its existence, has a profoundly intimate and personal character as far as Mary is concerned, and should therefore never be regarded by us as an impersonal relationship.

In receiving everything for the first time in faith for our sake, Mary was able to pass everything on to us. It is possible to state her function in this way by reference to St. Thomas's commentary on the Hail Mary: "What constitutes greatness in any saint is the extent to which the abundance of grace which he receives overflows for the salvation of many in the world. But, if any saint

[29] "Domine Jesu Christe, *noster apud Patrem mediator,* qui beatissimam Virginem matrem tuam, matrem quoque nostram, et *apud te mediatricem* constituere dignatus es: concede propitius; ut quisquis ad te beneficia petiturus accesserit, cuncta se per eam impetrasse laetetur."

were to receive sufficient grace for this to overflow for the salvation of all men in the world, this would be true greatness. This indeed exists in the case of Christ and the Blessed Virgin."[30] A super-abundance or overflow of grace is in itself a source of grace for others, since grace, as divine life, never has an exclusively individual significance: "Everyone must put the grace which is bestowed upon him at the service of his neighbour."[31] The basic difference between the superabundance of grace flowing from Christ and that which flows from Mary is to be found in the fact that Christ is, by definition, a man of grace. He is, in his manhood, the true Son of God. As man, then, he is God incarnate, naturally possessing divine life. That is why both St. Augustine and St. Thomas call Christ's grace a grace which is his "by nature."[32] His superabundance or overflow of grace is, therefore, the high tide of the only Mediator and Redeemer, who is both active and "sufficient in himself." Mary's superabundance of grace, on the other hand, is grace overflowing from her state of being both objectively and subjectively redeemed. It represents the peak of her participation in Christ's divine life. This flow of grace in us is the interior result of her state of being "universally redeemed," which in turn is due to Mary's divine motherhood. Her superabundance of grace, then, is the high tide of her *state of being redeemed*.

Viewed in this light, the title of "Suppliant Omnipotence" which Pope Pius XII bestowed on Mary may be said to comprise the entire mystery of Mary, in that she was, and still is, both suppliant and omnipotent. She is suppliant because her causality concerning the salvation of all men is based entirely upon her active receptivity

[30] Magnum est in quolibet sancto quando habet tantum de gratia quod sufficit ad salutem multorum. Sed quando haberet tantum quod sufficeret ad salutem *omnium hominum de mundo,* hoc esset maximum; et hoc est in Christo et in Beata Virgine." (*In Salutationem Angelicam, Opusc. Theol.* II, p. 240, no. 1118 in the Marietti edition.)

[31] "Quia quilibet de gratia sibi collata debet proximo inservire." (St. Thomas, *Expositio in Symbolum, Opusc. Theol.* II, p. 212, no. 975 in the Marietti edition.)

[32] St. Augustine, *Enchiridion,* c. 40 (*PL,* 40, col. 252); St. Thomas, *ST,* III, q. 2, a. 12.

with regard to Christ's work of redemption. She is at the same time omnipotent because of the depth of her pure receptivity with regard to God and her complete and *a priori* consent to God's omnipotence to save, which was manifested in Christ. In the first place, her spiritual reception and bodily conception of the most sublime gift of redemption, Christ himself as her own Child, constituted her complete avowal of Christ, her total acquiescence in the Father's will to redeem mankind by means of the saving event of the Incarnation and her free consent, in sacrificial love, to this divine saving event, not only at first, when she was scarcely aware of the far-reaching implications of this act, but also later, throughout the whole of her life on earth, when the full depths of these implications were slowly revealed to her. In the second place, this slowly developing inner awareness of her maternal function with regard to us, which became gradually clearer to her as the mystery of Christ, her Son, unfolded itself within history, led her to the point—especially at the foot of the Cross and at Pentecost—where her motherhood had become an essential, fully realized maternal relationship with regard to the entire Church and all men. Finally, in her glorified life in heaven, Mary is now perfectly conscious of her maternal function within the Christian plan of salvation and, living in a state of glorious, triumphant and sublimely active loving dedication and eternal receptivity, she is utterly at one, in will and intention, with the saving will and intention of the only saviour of mankind, Christ glorified. The term "mediation," first used in connection with Mary at the close of the patristic era by Byzantine theologians, adds nothing new to this threefold affirmation, and thus we must understand the term "mediatrix" in its light and not the other way round. This threefold affirmation is in fact equivalent to the recognition that Mary occupies an eminent position among all the redeemed by reason of her most intimate personal communion with the sole Mediator, Christ Jesus.

By virtue of the universal priority of her sublime *fiat,* as a free response to grace—in other words, on the basis of her universal merits here on earth which possessed an active priority over ours

—Mary, in her glorified state in heaven, must for us always remain a mystery of intercession and of maternal mediation. Her universal intercession on behalf of all men is one and the same phenomenon as her faithful consent to the Message, by which she merited redemption for us, in her own especially maternal way. Our prayers, our good works, our good intentions and our holiness—in a word, our free response to divine grace—are all comprised within the one great, prayerful *fiat* of the virgin mother of God. She is, as it were, ahead of us in every case of acceptance of faith, grace or life. She is the prototype of every instance of response to grace, and what she acquires for us, as the "Suppliant Omnipotence," is the need to respond, in faith and sacrificial love, to grace at all times in our lives. Mary is the universally receptive one, who always allows the Redeemer to bestow himself upon her and upon the whole of mankind. It is this quality which forms the basis of her prayer in heaven for all sinners, enabling us to call her the Refuge of Sinners. Her maternal solicitude for the salvation of all men, as the Help of Christians, is also based upon this quality. She is moreover the "honour and glory of our people"—by reason of her spiritual reception and bodily conception of the "Redeemer of our people" in a spirit of co-operative and utterly generous receptivity for our benefit.

3

THE DIVINE REASON FOR MARY'S PLACE IN THE PLAN OF SALVATION

WHY DID GOD CHOOSE MARY? What was his reason for giving her this particular place in his plan of salvation? This question synthesizes the entire Marian mystery. It forms the culminating point of the mystery and of the doctrine of Mary.

We have already indicated where Mary was situated, the precise place which she occupies in God's plan of salvation, but this does not, of course, mean that our examination of the subject of the mystery of Christ and Mary is complete. We have still to penetrate even further into the very heart of this mystery. It is certainly true that God's reason is God alone. This reason is first and foremost an aspect of God's boundless love for mankind. It is also a reason which is quite independent of any created situation or of any kind of "natural determinism." God's will is free from any "motive" which might move it either from within or from without, from any cause which might influence it or even from any inducement or postulated condition. His will exists in perfect, sovereign freedom and is, of its own nature, creative. God wills simply because he wills to will.

On the other hand, however, the God who so freely wills is good and omniscient. This means that any act of divine dispensation, in all its gratuitous freedom, is always a meaningful act. In the particular case which we are considering this not only resulted in Mary occupying the place assigned to her in the divine plan of salvation by God's will and at his discretion, but in this particular place at once becoming a meaningful moment in the whole economy of salvation. It is in this context that it is possible to refer to the divine motive for Mary's co-operation in the work of redemption.

The core of the whole Marian doctrine is contained in this question and, although the divine reason for the choice of Mary will always remain an unfathomable mystery, it is nonetheless possible to make its interior, implicit meaning to some extent explicit. This is the task which we shall attempt to accomplish in this chapter.

THE BASIC MARIOLOGICAL PRINCIPLE OF CONCRETE MOTHERHOOD, PERSONALLY ACCEPTED IN FAITH

Some Theological Views

One of the most useful of all the functions which the theologian can perform is, of course, to attempt to establish the organic connection which exists between the various mysteries of the Christian faith and, with particular reference to Mary, to make explicit, as far as he is able, the all-important and basic mystery. An explication of this basic mystery can make all the other mysteries intelligible within the context of faith and throw a clear light on the divine reason for the particular choice of Mary.

Before the Nestorian heresy, which denied Mary's divine motherhood, the Church Fathers tended to regard Mary principally as the "new Eve" and as the "prototype of the Church." It was not until the Council of Ephesus that her motherhood came to be regarded explicitly as the central mystery of Mary. This view has been maintained until the present century. Theologians, from Scheeben onwards, have, however, felt obliged to define this motherhood more precisely, by qualifying it with adjectives such as "bridal," "spiritual and bodily" or "adequate." This fact indicates quite clearly that motherhood in isolation cannot serve adequately as the basic principle in Mariology. In recent years many theologians have gone even further than this. Basing their claims on conclusions drawn from a close historical study of the earliest centuries, they have not only reaffirmed the patristic defini- tions—"Mary, the new Eve," "the prototype of the Church"—but have also proposed such definitions as "Mary, the prototype of redeemed mankind" and "the sublime firstfruit of the redemption." Definitions such as these, it is maintained, should form the basic principle of all teaching on the subject of Mary.

We should certainly welcome this renewed vision of Mary, which goes back to the first Fathers of the Church and once again places great emphasis on Mary's act of faith: "What the virgin Eve's lack of faith had bound was once more loosened by the faith of the Blessed Virgin Mary."[1] This concise statement ex- presses, in clear terms, a fundamental aspect of the teaching of the Church Fathers. What is more, this emphasis on Mary's act of faith does not, as we shall see, in any way affect the central position of her *concrete* motherhood.

Another reason why many theologians have felt compelled gradually to abandon Mary's motherhood as the basic Mariological principle is because they have found it very difficult to reconcile her virgin state with her later conversion to motherhood. If it is really impossible to find the organic connection between these two states, then it follows that the fundamental Mariological prin- ciple cannot be established solely on the basis of Mary's mother- hood.

Finally, some modern theologians have claimed that Mary's motherhood with regard to us cannot be reconciled with her mother- hood of Christ. Many have attempted to resolve their difficulties by basing Marian doctrine on *two* fundamental principles—Mary's motherhood and her participation in the Redemption. In their view, the two are sufficiently distinct from each other to be regarded as separate mysteries, but at the same time they were, at God's dis- cretion, embodied, and thus united, in one person.

[1] St. Irenaeus, *Adversus Haereses,* 3, 22, 4 (*PG,* 7, col. 959).

Mary's Spiritual and Bodily Concrete Motherhood;
the Anticipatory Sacramental Activity of This
Motherhood and Its Sacramental Consequences

We do not propose to go any further into the conceptualistic bias which underlies many of the views outlined in the foregoing paragraphs. Those who put forward such views assert that the "concept" of partnership or virginity is not included in the "concept" of motherhood. In making this claim, however, they forget that what we are dealing with here is a concrete reality which we can approach only imperfectly with our conceptual knowledge and thus explicate only very inadequately. What we propose to do here is to attempt to meet the various objections which have been put forward and then to proceed to state the basic Mariological principle in positive terms.

In the earlier part of this book we have tried to demonstrate how Mary's motherhood and her partnership in the Redemption were not so widely separate as many theologians claim. Keeping the concrete quality of her motherhood constantly in mind—Mary was governed in all things by God's dispensation and pleasure, and this did not result in the endowment, as it were from outside, of two distinctly separate attributes in one and the same person— we are bound to recognize that Mary, as the mother of Christ, who was the representative of the whole of mankind, had at least some degree of relationship, because of this, with the whole of mankind to be redeemed. Furthermore, it must also be clear that the Incarnation was, in the *concrete* sense, a redemptive incarnation and that Mary's *fiat,* her agreeing to become the mother of the Messiah, was at the same time an implicit *fiat* to the redemptive sacrifice of the Cross. Her co-suffering at the foot of the Cross was the explicit continuation of her express *fiat* to motherhood— a developed aspect of her freely accepted concrete motherhood.

We have shown earlier on that Mary's virgin state and her motherhood are not two separate mysteries, existing as it were side by side, but that hers was a virgin motherhood, that it was as a virgin that she was a mother. We have already seen, too, how, as a consequence of this, Mary's virginity indicates a very real aspect, not only of her motherhood (with regard to Christ and to us) but also of her freely accepted motherhood in the concrete sense.

Finally, the particular emphasis upon the proposition that the basic Mariological principle is to be found in Mary as the prototype of the Church enables us to define more precisely the view set out in the earlier part of this chapter.

Mary's *fiat,* upon which the early Fathers placed so much stress, and her motherhood, so prominent in all Marian doctrine from the Council of Ephesus right up to the present day, are not two distinctly separate mysteries. They imply, on the one hand, a concrete motherhood, freely accepted in faith, which at the same time coincides identically with Mary's objective and subjective, exceptional and unique state of being redeemed. Hers was in no way an abstract motherhood. It was essentially and in every way concrete. Mary was, on the other hand, also the "sublimely redeemed" in the most complete sense, and she was thus sublimely redeemed by virtue of the fact that she was predestined to enjoy the fundamental privilege of her motherhood. To express this idea in another way, she was on the one hand sublimely redeemed, both objectively and subjectively, in, through and because of her concrete motherhood with regard to Christ; on the other hand, she became the mother of the concrete Christ in, through and because of the exceptional and profound quality of her *fiat.* The two ways of looking at the mystery are implicit in each other, though each is on a different level.

Human motherhood is not merely a biological function. The biological function of motherhood implies a personal and free commitment on the part of the mother. In Mary's case this free, personal involvement in motherhood meant that she freely and personally took upon herself a saving function which bound her both spiritually and physically, in the most intimate manner, to the God-man Christ, the head of the whole of mankind which he had come to redeem, and consequently to all of us. Mary's personal commitment—her sublime consent made in faith—and her motherhood were thus essentially related to each other. Her exceptional submission in faith was therefore, essentially and intrinsically, directed towards the exceptional offer of redemption made in the person of Christ, as the child of her own womb. Her motherhood, on the one hand, and her personal, sublime state of redeemed holiness, on the other, cannot be conceived in isolation from each other. Each is implied in the other, and this essential relationship existing between the two entitles us to claim that it is Mary's concrete motherhood which constitutes the fundamental principle of the entire mystery of Mary. Her concrete motherhood with regard to Christ, the redeeming God-man, freely accepted in faith—her fully committed divine motherhood—this is both the key to a full understanding of the Marian mystery and the basic Mariological principle, which is concretely identical with Mary's objectively and subjectively unique state of being redeemed.

In this way too, it is possible to achieve a reconciliation between the strong emphasis which the Church Fathers before the Council of Ephesus placed upon Mary's *fiat,* and the prominence given to her divine motherhood in the traditional thought of the Church since the Council. Moreover, those modern theologians, on the one hand, who tend to situate the basic Mariological principle in Mary as the prototype of the Church, the new Eve or the sublimely redeemed, also tend to overlook the fact that the entire content and meaning of Mary's *fiat,* of her holiness and of her state of redemption, are determined objectively by the vital content of the Message: motherhood with regard to the Redeemer.

On the other hand, however, those who subscribe to the older view, which accepted Mary's motherhood as the basic principle, tend to see this motherhood in too abstract terms and even, in extreme cases, simply in terms of its purely biological function. The essential aspect of Mary's personal commitment in faith to the full implications of her motherhood is bound to be neglected in a onesided view of this kind. Finally, the other modern tendency, that of accepting a double Mariological principle of motherhood and partnership, also overemphasizes an abstract concept of motherhood and ignores the concrete implications contained in Mary's concrete motherhood with regard to Christ, the God-man, who was by vocation the head of the mankind he was called to redeem.

Mary, then, may be regarded both as "objectively and subjectively sublimely redeemed" and as the subject of "freely accepted and personally committed motherhood with regard to the Redeemer." These two basic principles of Marian doctrine are different in formulation and particular accentuation, but fundamentally identical. It should therefore be possible to relate organically all the Marian mysteries both to the fundamental privilege of the "sublimely redeemed" and to the same, but differently formulated, privilege of "concrete, freely accepted motherhood," even though, concerning the former privilege, we have to bear in mind that the sublimity of Mary's objective and subjective redemption derives its concrete significance from her motherhood. Pope Pius XII showed that he fully accorded with the most profound tradition of faith when he called Mary's divine motherhood the foundation of all her privileges.

Taken in connection with the foregoing argument, our view can best be expressed in the following way. Mary was the Chosen One. She was redeemed by her immensely deep *fiat* made in faith, externally represented in her bodily *conception* of the universal primordial sacrament, the holy man Jesus Christ, the God-man. She was, in other words, redeemed by her motherhood, insofar as it was fully accepted as a personal and free commitment on the part of the mother. Mary's immaculate conception, the holy state in which she lived before the Message, her exemption from sin and sinful desires, her entire relationship with and attitude towards God, in virgin dedication as the "handmaid of the Lord"—all this was anticipatory sacramental activity, preceding her conception in faith (*fide concepit*) of the primordial sacrament, Christ.

On the other hand, all that followed this conception—her spiritual motherhood with regard to us, her specific share, as Mary, in the Redemption, her co-meritorious mediatorship of all graces, her universal intercession and finally her early physical glorification and her "constitution in power"—all this constituted subsequent sacramental efficacy. Thus the mystery of Mary, Christ's most beautiful creation, emerges as an organic mystery, based on the fundamental privilege of concrete motherhood freely accepted in faith. It is this privilege which provides us with the key to a full understanding, in faith, of the entire mystery of Mary.

It is possible to approach this mystery from two different points of view. On the one hand, if our point of departure is faith as the inspiration of every sacramental reception, we are bound to proceed from Mary's subjective redemption or free commitment in faith in order to arrive at the point where we can see how her personal appropriation of objective redemption was determined and given a specific meaning, peculiar to herself, by her mother-hood. If we consider the mystery from this point of view, we are bound to accept, as our basic Mariological principle, that Mary is the new Eve, the prototype of the Church and of every redeemed life.

It is, on the other hand, possible to take the objective sacra-mental gift as the starting-point from which to approach the mystery of Mary. In this case we are bound to proceed from Mary —her bodily conception of Christ—in order to throw light upon her subjective participation in her own redemption and in that of all men.

These two different ways of considering the mystery are not mutually exclusive, since a true sacrament, in the fullest sense of the word—that is, a fruitful sacrament—contains in itself both a reception in faith and a total submission in hope and love.

This is why a comprehensive Marian doctrine, which aims to bring all the mysteries of Mary together into a single, organic whole under one basic Mariological principle, must at the same time always take both the objective and the subjective aspects of redemption into full consideration. The essential core of the Marian mystery is that she conceived in faith (*fide concepit*), that her motherhood was one to which she freely committed herself in faith. The mystery can consequently be seen as a concrete, though exceptional and singular, case of "objective and subjective redemption" affecting one particular and special child of Adam. Because the heart and centre of Mary's unique quality is to be found in her motherhood, she, though *within* redeemed humanity, was at the same time infinitely elevated above the community of her co-redeemed fellows. She is therefore not only our sister but also our mother, the mother of the "whole Christ, both head and members," the mother of the Creator, the "fully committed" and therefore maternal mother of the omnipotent Creator of the universe.

THE MOTHER IN THE CHURCH AND MOTHER
OF ALL PEOPLE

The Divine Reason for Mary's Election

In the earlier part of this book we have shown that Mary's activity is only conceivable within the context of the redemption brought by Christ alone, but that Mary, as the Mother of God, was nonetheless endowed with a universal saving function within this plan of salvation which only she could fulfil by reason of her maternal quality, her bodily conception and spiritual receptivity. It was God's will that this maternal quality should play an essential part in his dispensation of grace. In this sense, Mary's state of being Christ's and our mother explicates something of Christ's redemption, an element which is not explicated itself in Christ's act of redemption and which even cannot be explicated in this act. This is the feminine and maternal quality of goodness.

The goodness of God's redemptive love is both paternal and maternal. "I have loved thee with an everlasting love," we read in the Old Testament. (Jer. 31. 3.) The prophet Hosea describes the maternal love of Yahweh for his people: "When Israel was a child, I loved him. It was I who taught Ephraim to walk, I carried them in my arms: and they knew not that I healed them. I drew them to me with human cords, with the bands of love. I pressed them to my cheek like a nurse, bent over them to feed them." (Hos. 11. 1 ff.) In Isaiah too we find expression of the maternal love of Yahweh: "Can a woman forget her infant, so as not to have pity on the son of her womb? And if she should forget, yet will I not forget thee. Behold, I have graven thee in my hands." (Isa. 49. 15–16.) In this last passage the prophet compares Yahweh to a betrothed virgin who, according to the custom of the times, has inscribed the name of her beloved on the palm of her hand. God, too, has written our names on the palm of his hand so that he will always be mindful of his loved ones.

These texts certainly indicate that God's love for mankind, as manifested in the Redeemer, is really a maternal love. This maternal quality of mildness, this particularly feminine tenderness, this *quid nesciam* which is the special mark of the mother cannot, however, be explicated as such in the man Jesus. It can only become explicit in a mother who is a woman. God chose Mary so that this maternal aspect of his love might be represented in her person. At the deepest level this would seem to be the basic reason why a woman, a mother, should have a role in the Redemption. Mary's activity is essentially a maternal function.

We may, however, be quite certain that Mary's saving intervention is beyond all doubt perfectly attuned to Christ and that it detracts in no way from his unique function as Redeemer. We should not lose sight of the fact that her virginity forms an essential part of her quality as a mother. She is a *virgin* woman and mother. As such, her love for her children is never demanding or possessive. Never does she claim their love for herself. The sole object of her virgin maternal love is to lead her children to the love of Christ. All her motherly care is directed towards Christ.

It would be possible to quote a thousand instances from the lives of the saints in illustration of Mary's virgin motherly love which always seeks to orientate her children's love towards Christ. All of us must also, at some time or another, be aware of it in our own lives. Many great sinners too, who have lost their faith in Christ, still remain open to the tenderness which is apparent in "Mother Mary" and, in spite of everything, never cease to be "children of Mary." It is always possible, as long as they remain open to Mary, that they may perhaps find Christ again, in the nick of time. Another example of this is the characteristic tenderness of Catholic devotion, as opposed to the comparative severity of Protestant Christianity. It is, of course, true that a race or people, as for example those of the Mediterranean countries, may give their own particular shape or colour to Catholic practice, and that this may be, and frequently is, due rather to a hybrid than to a pure form of Marian devotion. But at the same time no one can possibly deny that Catholic devotion as such is marked by a tenderness, a mildness, even a childlike and loving simplicity —and the only adequate explanation for this is that the Catholic grows up in faith in the intimate company of the most loving and lovable of all mothers, the *Mater Amabilis,* the Virgin with the Smile.

Growing up in close intimacy with Mother Mary, the Catholic learns the meaning of generosity from the boundless and indeed almost wasteful goodness of Mary, who surrounds every offering, even the ultimate sacrifice of Christ—for Christ on the Cross was still above all the true Child of Mary and felt the soothing balm of his mother's love during his crucifixion—with her infinite tenderness and makes life easier and more bearable for the Christian. Christ's "yoke is not heavy"—it cannot be disputed that Mary has a part to play in lightening the Christian's burden. It is surely not surprising that the cry which comes spontaneously to the Christian's lips when he is in need is "Mary." She it is who enables us to participate in Christ's sacrifice in a spirit of *gentle* submission. The creator of all goodness, the blessed Trinity who sent the Second Person to redeem us, and decreed that he should be born, in the real sense, as Mary's Child, had a profound knowledge and understanding of the human heart! It is only if we consider Christ and his mother together that we can fully grasp the idea of the "gentleness" of the Cross.

Seen in this light, the Redemption, in its fully human sense, is traceable not solely to the God-man, but also to the virgin, feminine and maternal quality of the mother of the God-man. This perspective also enables us to see the Christian redemption as the highest exaltation of humanity. The Redemption, accomplished by God himself by way of human nature, is fully human because it was given to us by the man Jesus and his and our mother. Woman played an essential part in the first sin and the Fall. The new Eve fulfilled a sublimely feminine function in the plan of redemption. "Male and female he created them." Mary is the *dulcedo,* the sweetness in Christianity: "Our life, our sweetness."

Mary was Jesus' mother. This means that Jesus, as a man, was brought up by Mary and Joseph. This is, of course, a great mystery and difficult for the human mind to grasp. Nonetheless, we must affirm the dogma that Christ was a true human being and, as such, had to be brought up and educated, in the strictest sense of the word, by his mother. His human qualities and character were formed and influenced by his mother's virtues. And when we read in Scripture that Christ went around in the land of Palestine doing good, and realize that this human goodness was God's love of men translated into human terms, we are bound to acknowledge too that Mary had a maternal share in this Christian interpretation of God's love. It is common human experience that the mother's features are recognizable in the child, and this was also true in the case of Mary and Jesus. Mary's function in the Incarnation was not completed when Jesus was born. It was a continuous task, involving the human formation of the young man, as he grew up from infancy to childhood and from childhood to adulthood. How this was accomplished is hidden from us. Only Mary knew the secrets of Jesus' upbringing, and kept them in her heart. She, his mother, kept the secret of the first childish word her Child ever spoke to her and meditated it in her heart. God, in his humanity, formed his first word, and there can be little doubt that it was "Mama."

Theologians are always anxious to tie down Mary's maternal activity and reduce it to theological formulae. They like to measure her share in the Redemption accurately and compare it in minute detail with Christ's redemptive activity. But how could you possibly answer me, if I were to ask: "On whom can family life be said ultimately to depend—on the father or on the mother?" It would be quite impossible to give a clearly defined answer to this question. In the family the relationships between father and mother are so delicately interwoven that the individual parts played by both parents can never be precisely divided and accounted for separately. Father and mother are indivisibly united, and what God has joined together, man may not put asunder. The good father is always intimately affected by the nearness and activity of the mother. The mother is entirely absorbed in everything that the father does and is trying to do. She looks up to him in admiration and shares his life, doing what he does together with him in her own maternal way. The mother's influence so permeates the whole of the family's life that it can even be felt in an empty room. She is an atmosphere, but an atmosphere that is always active and busy. She influences all those who live and breathe in this atmosphere.

Something of this kind happens in the life of their family, which is the Church. Christ and Christ alone—and God in humanity—was responsible for everything, but, within the Holy Family, Mary became Christ's maternal partner, with the result that everything that happened in the family was affected by her maternal quality. Viewed in this light, we may also say that Mary too was responsible for everything, as the Mother of the Redeemer and of his redemption. Christ's redemption was offered to us by Christ in his Church, saturated, as it were, with this maternal quality. All Mary's being, all her activity, then, amounted to this: as a mother, she constantly converted into maternal terms everything that Christ thought, desired, felt and did concerning our salvation. This process of conversion is, of course, still continuing. Mary is the translation and effective expression in maternal terms of God's mercy, grace and redeeming love which manifested itself to us in a visible and tangible form in the person of Christ, our Redeemer. She derived her maternal power from being so close to Christ, her own Child, her and our Redeemer, who emanated power. This is in no way different from Christ's normal activity, but in Mary's case it contained a unique and irreplaceable element, since it involved her participation as his mother.

This can also help us to understand the dogmatic development of the Marian mystery. The concrete reality, expressed in utter simplicity by the bare scriptural fact "Mary, the mother of Jesus," comprises the entire dogma of Mary. All the other definitions of faith concerning Mary merely serve to develop or set out in greater detail what is contained in this infinitely rich concrete motherhood.

To be a mother is, however, not simply a momentary fact—bearing a child. It is a long process of growth and development lasting the whole of life, in which full and mature motherhood is attained only as a result of the continuous action and reaction which takes place between the mother and the child. We should, therefore, avoid thinking of Mary's motherhood with regard to Christ, and consequently of her spiritual motherhood with regard to all of us, as an act of faith and love which occupied no more than a single moment of time. Mary's motherhood was a progressive reality. Bearing in mind what has been said in the foregoing paragraphs, we can outline Mary's maternal development schematically as follows.

Her immaculate conception and virgin life prepared her for her later pure motherhood and her maternal activity in the service of the Kingdom of God. Her assent to the angel's message made her in the real sense the mother of the God-man, our Redeemer, and thus at once the spiritual mother of the whole of mankind awaiting Christ's redemption. Her maternal communion with her crucified Child, our Redeemer, made her at once the tender mother of the whole of redeemed humanity. As a result of her Pentecost experience, she acquired a mature awareness of her maternal task within the redeemed world. Finally, her assumption into heaven and her spiritual and physical glorification made her queen and mother. Now, as the glorified mother, she is "in power." Enjoying the beatific vision granted to her by the glorified Christ, she has a clear, intuitive consciousness of her maternal task and knows all men intimately in their individual circumstances and their concrete worries and cares. In heaven she is concerned for every one of them and uses her maternal love on their behalf, so that the kingdom of her Son may be fulfilled.

What we really mean, when we refer to Mary as the co-redemptrix, the mediatrix of all graces, or the one who dispenses grace and intercedes for all men, is nothing more or less than this: She is "in power" as the glorified mother of the redemption brought by Christ alone, the mother who completely identifies herself, in maternal love, with the redemptive acts of her Child, our Redeemer. In other words, within the Communion of Saints, the Mother of Jesus enjoys the most intimate human communion with the sole Redeemer. The various titles given to Mary are but other expressions of this one fundamental reality. On the basis of this same reality, moreover, all these titles are reduced to their proportions.

The Church reveals the inexpressible wealth of the enormous reality contained in the image of the "mother of the redeemer of the world" only in separate statements. The basic structural lines of this image of Mary, the mother, the first lines from which this portrait has been built up, have emerged only very slowly with the passage of time. We have now reached the stage where nothing remains to be discovered as far as the basic structure is concerned. We shall, however, never come to the end of our search for the content and meaning of the essential maternal features of the image. This is surely comparable to our experience at the purely human level—our insight into the nature of our own mother here on earth deepens as we grow older and our gradual understanding of her as our mother discloses new horizons of which we were not explicitly conscious during our early life. Scripture and the Apostles' understanding of "Mary, the mother of Jesus" provided the basis for an intuition which has become more and more clear with the passage of time in the Church's life of faith. The later dogmatic pronouncements of the Church can thus be regarded as joyous words which have been suggested to us while what we were unable to express was on the tip of our tongues. In this way the holy possession which had hitherto been latent was able to achieve a greater clarity. "Behold thy mother"—these words from the Cross form, as it were, Christ's dogmatic definition which the Church has since broken down, analytically, into richly varied, separate dogmas.

Catholics should have no cause to be astonished at the apparently tremendous development from the Gospel image to the dogmatic vision of Mary. The basic reason for the difference between the Protestant and the Catholic attitudes towards Mary in the sphere of worship is undoubtedly to be found in the different dogmatic views of Christ and in the fact that we, as Catholics, do not hesitate to call our Lady the mother of the redeeming God in humanity. Our Protestant brothers in faith, on the other hand, do not appear to grasp the deep and fundamental meaning of this great reality, "God in humanity," and consequently fail to fathom the full depths of Mary's motherhood. At the same time, they misinterpret her essential maternal quality, by denying man's personal, meritorious co-operation in his salvation. This particular misconception is probably the cause of their further misunderstanding of Mary's true greatness and sublime place in the event of the Incarnation. The characteristically Protestant attitude towards Mary, then, not only colours the Protestant's dogmatic vision of faith. It also forms the basis of Protestant, as distinct from Catholic, spirituality.

Mother in the Church and Mother of All

Although the question of Mary's motherhood of all people has, fundamentally, been answered in the foregoing section, it is necessary for us to reconsider the entire topic in another light, that of Mary and the Church, since the problem of Mary, as the type of the Church, is to some extent emphasized in contemporary Mariology. An examination of this aspect of Mary's function should also throw some light on the place which Mary occupies in our sacramental "subjective redemption."

The concrete sense of the Incarnation is to be found in the fact that, in his redemptive activity, the God-man is, by vocation, the representative of the human race. In this sense, Christ is himself, representatively, the Church. The sacrifice of the Cross is the sacrifice of the whole of humanity—"objective redemption" is to be found precisely in this fact. The Church was born on the Cross.[2]

Nevertheless, redemption has still to be accomplished *in us*. Universal membership of the Church, made possible for all men by Christ's sacrifice, has still to be made a reality in the personal sense. It is in this sense that the Church is the community of the faithful who, inspired by the Holy Ghost, allow themselves, in hope and love, to be seized by the redemptive act brought about by the living Christ and rally round him. The members of this Church form the new People of God. Seen in this light, the Church is the *congregatio fidelium*, the community of grace and faith, composed of all those who belong to Christ and hope for the glorious *parousia* of the Lord.

But, since what is at stake here is the salvation of human beings, this community is also bound to be a visible community. Man's social character would certainly form a natural basis for the Church as a visible community. All the same, it does not, in the *concrete* sense, provide the foundation of the visible community of the Church. As a visible community of grace in Christ, the Church is not constructed, as it were, from ground level upwards, but from above—from the highest point downwards. The Church comes from Christ himself. The heavenly Christ continues his work of redemption among us in a separate religious community established by him here on earth. He perpetuates his redemptive work in the Word and in the sacramental life of the Church.

---

[2] "Moritur Christus ut fiat Ecclesia." (St. Augustine, *In Joh. Evan.*, tract. 9, no. 10: see also the papal encyclical *Mystici Corporis*, in *AAS* [1953], p. 204.)

The Church—and this also includes the Church's hierarchical structure—is the visible extension on earth of Christ, invisible in heaven. Christ's work of redemption is made visibly present for us in and through the Church, that is, in word and sacrament, in order that we should be personally confronted by it.

The apostolic office—the ecclesiastical hierarchy—was entrusted with the word and the sacrament. Christ established the first principles of the hierarchical structure of the Church as a community of faith, in the word, the sacrament and the apostolic office, before the Church existed as a community of believers. "The Apostles and their successors are God's [Christ's] deputies in the administration of the Church which was brought about by faith and the sacraments of the faith."[3]

The Church may, then, be regarded as Christ both visible and sacramental. Viewed in this way, she has a double function: (1) She is the visible sacramentalization of the heavenly Christ, by means of which he is able to bring about the community of faith and love—the Church as a community of grace—on earth. During Jesus' earthly life, any encounter with the living God was a sacramental encounter with the man Jesus, by virtue of the fact that this encounter was created in and through the holy and efficacious sign of Jesus' humanity. In precisely the same way, we are able to encounter God after Christ's ascension in the external, visible Church, in which Christ's sacred humanity comes to meet us in a sacramental manner. The Church is a sanctifying community. (2) She is at the same time the visible expression, the making visible, of the inward community of faith and love of all those who are baptized in Christ. In this sense the Church is a community of worship.

The inward community of grace and the outward sacramental organism together form the single mystical body of Christ.

This Church is referred to as our Mother. It is, however, of interest that, historically speaking, the Church was called our Mother before Mary was given this title. Nonetheless, it was the idea of Mary's motherhood which inspired that of the motherhood

[3] St. Thomas, *Summa Theol.*, III, q. 64, a. 2, ad 3.

of the Church. The Church was originally called our Mother as a result of this implicit feeling for Mary as the mother of all the redeemed. This gives a clear indication of the fact that the Church Fathers, almost unconsciously, tended to regard the Church, in the first centuries of Christianity, through the figure of the Mother of God.

Mary, the type of the redeemed community of the Church.—As the Chosen People, the Jews formed the type of the new Israel or the Church. The divine saving intention which this truth conceals is that mankind itself has, in a spirit of love, to make a gift to the redeeming God of its humanity—that same humanity in and through which God has in fact redeemed us from within. The redeeming God has in fact worked this out himself in human history, by effecting a history of salvation within mankind's history of disaster. The living God has more than once lovingly entered human history in order to reverse man's sinful history by means of his grace and to change its course by a saving act. In the first place, he initiated a process of selection. Choosing one man from the whole of the human race—Abram—he put his faith to the test, with the aim of making him the first ancestor, the father of a chosen race through which salvation would be brought into the world. This selective process became more clearly defined with the passage of time, until the idea of the God "who was to come" gradually crystallized in men's minds. Eventually the "Chosen Race" became identified with the one person—the virgin from Nazareth. Mankind, informed by grace, moved gradually towards the fullness of time, and this movement can be seen as a process of purification which achieved its most noble expression in the person of the *Immaculata*. Mary was the exponent of the Chosen Race, the Jewish people, which in turn was itself the type of the Church which was to come. In this way, she was the point of contact between the Old Covenant and the New.[4]

The culminating point of man's expectations of the Messiah thus

---

[4] "Dicendum quod beata Virgo fuit confinium Veteris et Novae Legis, sicut aurora diei et noctis." (St. Thomas, *In IV Sent.*, d. 30, q. 2, a. 1, sol. 1, ad 1.)

coincided with the climax of the realization of these messianic hopes. Mary, who was the most receptive of all the Chosen Race, became the most richly endowed with gifts in the Kingdom of Heaven. It was in Mary that what the prophet Hosea dreamed of concerning God's chosen people came to pass—God's spotless bride. (Hos. 2. 14–24.) The mediatory function which the Jewish people, as the vehicle of God's universal promise to save all men, fulfilled, was concentrated in the Jewish girl, Mary. She was the Daughter of Zion personified. One characteristic feature of many of the titles given to Mary in the Litany of the Blessed Virgin should not be overlooked. Such titles as Ark of the Covenant, Door of Heaven, Refuge of Sinners, Tower of David and so on were initially applied to Israel and the Church, and only later to Mary. The mystery of the Church and that of Mary have always thrown light upon each other.

This mediatory function for the salvation of mankind was purely the work of God's elective love: *Elegit eam Deus et praeelegit eam.* On the other hand, however, an election of this kind was bound to impose tremendous conditions, by which Mary's special function could at the same time become, as it were, the result of a sacrificial total involvement in faith of exceptional depth on the part of the one who was chosen to be the firstfruit of his or her people and to lead it towards salvation. This unconditional sacrificial faith on the part of the man elected to be the father of the Chosen People or the woman chosen to become the mother of the human race was an absolute necessity. The People of God is first and foremost a community of believers, and this must appear as "typical" in the faith of the person in whom the vocation of the entire people is personified. This unconditional faith is the first condition both of the promise and of the fulfilment of this promise. This fact emerges very clearly from the three "typical" cases of Adam, Abraham and Mary.

(1) The first "type" of religious mankind failed. We are told, in the primitive account of Adam's history, how the faith of the "first man" was put to the test. Had he emerged successfully from this test

of his faith, a blessing would have been conferred, in him, upon the whole of mankind. The apparently arbitrary character of God's sovereign commandment, expressed in the statement that the fruit of one tree might be eaten, whereas the fruit of another was forbidden (whatever may have been the real content of the precept), proved to be the stumbling-block for Adam's faith. He failed to surrender unconditionally to sacrificial faith. Adam's disbelief, then, made him the "type" of fallen humanity. In him we all became sinners.

(2) "Can I hide from Abraham what I am about to do: seeing he shall become a great and mighty nation, and in him all the nations of the earth shall be blessed?" (Gen. 18. 17–18.) The condition for the realization in history of this election was, again, a test of faith. Yahweh had told Abram that he was to leave his home and take his barren wife to a land which his future offspring would inherit. After a long time had elapsed, Abraham became a little uneasy and began to wonder whether God would in fact keep his promise. God repeated his promise to Abraham that his barren wife would eventually bear a child, at the same time stressing the importance of Abraham's continuing belief in this promise. Abraham, however, did what so many men who do not possess the patience of God do in such cases—he looked for immediate results at the human level. He had a child, not by his wife Sarah, but by the handmaid Hagar. According to Mesopotamian law, this child, Ishmael, was Abraham's legal heir. God, however, thought differently, and renewed his promise. In his patience he was not angry with Abraham and Sarah for their laughter and lack of faith. Eventually, however, Abraham learned to believe in God's repeated, insistent statement: "Is there anything hard to God?" (Gen. 18. 14), and at last Isaac was born to Sarah in her old age—the "laughter" which dispelled the original unbelief. (Cf. Gen. 17. 17–19.) Now it was God's turn to laugh in triumph.

This did not, however, mean that God's testing of Abraham's faith was at an end, for Abraham's surrender was still not absolutely unconditional. God gave him, as it were, a fresh chance, since, however relentless his demands may be, God never simply provokes his creatures. The second test came when Isaac was still a young man—God commanded Abraham to sacrifice this son of his promise.[5] Against all hope, Abraham nonetheless trusted in God, and after this final test of his faith became, through faith in what was humanly impossible, the ancestor of the Chosen People and the type of the religious community of Israel, the foreshadowing of the Church. Abram had become Abraham.

(3) The mother of the new community of faith also underwent a similar paradoxical test of faith. She was to become the mother of the royal Messiah. We have already seen, in the first chapter of this book, how Mary's faith was constantly confronted by apparent contradictions and how she nonetheless continued to believe in the staggering mystery. The special test of her faith was, of course, when her Son, to whom, according to the Message, had been given the promise of an imperishable kingdom, died on the Cross without any apparent hope of rescue. This was Mary's sacrifice of Abraham, but in her case no angel came at the last moment to prevent the effective total offering from taking place. God demanded a total unconditional surrender on her part to the mystery. Thus Mary became the mother of the new People of God ransomed by Christ by means of her *cooperatio caritatis*,[6] and through her unconditional maternal sacrificial faith and love.

The one, chosen out of the many in the human community, was redeemed in order to become the first fruit of the Redemption. That is to say, she was redeemed in order that she might, as a mother, represent in her own person and in a "typical" manner what the whole of the Church was to be—virgin fidelity to Christ and maternal fruitfulness. In this context, what St. Paul had to say concerning the Church and Christ's relationship with the Church is strictly pertinent: "Christ also loved the Church and delivered himself up

---

[5] Whatever the historical meaning of this account may be—Abraham's abrogation of the sacrifice of the eldest son—a deeper significance was read into the event later on. See also St. Paul, Rom. 4. 1–22.

[6] St. Augustine, *De S. Virg.*, 6, 6 (*PL*, 40, col. 399).

for it; that he might sanctify it and cleanse it . . . that he might present it to himself, a glorious church, not having spot or wrinkle . . . but that it should be holy and without blemish." (Eph 5. 25–7.) Christ fully realized this, in the first place, in his mother Mary. The entire life of the Church throughout her history is nothing more nor less than a growth, an ascent, towards the image of the Mother of God.

What has been fully accomplished in Mary is still in a process of growth and becoming in the Church on earth. The *parousia*—the glorification and the spiritual and bodily togetherness of redeemed man with Christ in triumph—has already taken place for Mary and for Mary alone. In the words of St. Thomas, "The true Church, our Mother, is in heaven; we grow up towards her, and the entire reality of the Church Militant [on earth] is to be found in her conformity with the Church in heaven."[7] The spotless Virgin Mother, which is the Church, is an eschatological reality, a vision of a future heavenly reality. This reality has, however, already been accomplished in the *Assumpta,* although on earth the Church, our Virgin Mother, is still on pilgrimage. In this sense Mary makes the Church on earth a real Church, since the heavenly Church is, according to St. Thomas, the *true* Church from which the Church on earth is derived, and may be called a *real* Church.

Mary is therefore the prototype of the whole Church. Until now, it is only in her that the Church is in the fullest sense Church. The word *tupos*—type or prototype—which the Fathers of the Church use in this context, does not simply mean an example, a pattern or a model. It refers first and foremost to a human figure, a person from whose personal life-history or career and from whose ultimate state God's design to save his chosen people may clearly emerge. God clearly manifests his intentions concerning the Church in the perfect image of the Virgin Mother. The word "type" does not, moreover, refer exclusively to a static image to which we should look up—a model which we should admire and upon which we should fashion our lives. It refers rather to something much more

[7] St. Thomas, *In ad Ephes.,* c. 3, lect. 3.

dynamic—a saving power. It should show us that Mary, as the "type" of the Church, personally consecrated herself to the task of helping to bring about in the other members of the Church community what had already been "typically" realized in her life by Christ. Since she is, as a mother, the type of the Church, she is able to co-operate maternally in the work of the Church built up and extended by Christ. Only in this sense can she be called "Mother of the Church," that is, the Church owes her proper maternal character to Mary.

We are therefore bound to acknowledge the truth of St. Augustine's statement, "Mary is a part of the Church, a holy member, an excellent and prominent member, but still a *member* of the whole Church."[8] But *in* the Church she is the spiritual and physical womb of the Church. It should be possible, then, to define Mary's relationship to the Church more precisely from this point onwards.

Mary's place in the Church community of grace and her relation to the sacramental and hierarchical Church.—In any comparison between Mary, the Virgin Mother, and the *Virgo et Mater Ecclesia,* it is imperative for us to bear in mind one fundamental distinction.

In calling Mary the prototype of the Church, it is necessary to distinguish between that aspect of the Church which we have characterized as the community of grace and that other aspect, the Church regarded as a sacramental, hierarchical institution. Mary can be considered as the type of the Church only in its first aspect. Indeed, she forms the culminating point of the community of grace with Christ in the Church. Her grace is the highest ideal in the redeemed Christian life. Such a high tide, such a flood of grace also contains a universal power, capable of exerting an influence over all men and capable, what is more, of doing this in a manner peculiar to this particular and sublime subject of grace. The influence exercised by this universal power of grace is a purely maternal influence, springing from and following the course of a mother's love. The grace which stems from the sacramental, hierarchical Church is, on the other hand, of a sacerdotal kind and is not in

[8] *Sermo XXV de Verbis Evang. Matth. XII. XLI–L (PL,* 46, col. 938).

any way due to Mary, since she does not form part of the ranks of the Church's hierarchy. Mary is not a priestess.

This is, however, not to say that the grace conferred by the sacraments is entirely outside Mary's influence. The grace given to us by the sacraments is always Christ's grace, and Christ was and is, as we have seen, imbued with Mary's maternal qualities. The Church, which, as the visible community, perpetuates the work of our redemption and distributes redemptive grace among us in an institutional manner, thus mediates the grace which was acquired by Christ and co-acquired maternally by Mary. We should not infer that there is something lacking in Mary because she forms no part of the sacramental Church as a structural principle. On the contrary, her not belonging to the sacramental Church as a structural principle results from the fact that she already fulfilled an essential and maternal function at the very inception of the redemptive act. The sacramental Church fulfils the function of communicating this redemption to us.

In this sense the whole of the Church's sacramental activity in the mediation of grace, considered as an act of Christ who is received by men in faith and love, can be seen to be foreshadowed in Mary's life. In faith she did not receive a specific sacrament, but the Primordial Sacrament itself, Jesus Christ in person. Mary's reception of the sacrament, anticipating both in time and in order of importance every subsequent case of personal reception, in the Church, of a specific sacrament, constitutes the prototype of the sacramental life of the Church, as seen from the point of view of the subject or recipient. In the words of Leo the Great, "The principle of birth which Christ found in Mary's womb has been embodied by him in the water of baptism: *Dedit aquae quod dedit matri*. The power of the Most High and the overshadowing of the Holy Ghost, which brought about the birth of the Redeemer in the Virgin Mary, also make it possible for the water of baptism to bring about a rebirth in the faithful."[9]

Christ alone and, in his power, the sacramental Church, are the

[9] *Sermo XXV*, 4 (*PL*, 54, col. 211).

ministers of the sacraments. Mary is not. She is on the side of those who receive the sacraments. Christ, however, is the principal minister of the sacraments, and the hierarchical Church distributes the sacraments in his power and is subordinate to him, as his servant, administering the sacraments through her priests. In precisely the same way, Mary, who personally received the Primordial Sacrament in sublime faith and love, is the principal recipient, and we receive the sacraments in her actively receptive power. In this sense, Mary is completely outside the priestly distribution of the sacraments, although the hierarchical aspect of the Church is fully included in her universal, maternal and saving mediation. Her relationship towards the saving power of the sacraments can therefore provide us, if we consider it within the context of the sacramental communication of the grace acquired by Christ, with a clear understanding of Christ's unique position as the only Redeemer and Mary's maternal self-identification with Christ's work of salvation. The direct consequence of this is that Christ's grace is at the same time always Mary's, our maternal advocate's grace.

Although I find it a less attractive way of describing the relationship, it is also possible to say that Mary is outside what we might call the technique of the sacraments, though not outside the life of the sacraments. It seems to me to be a fundamental misconception to situate Mary, in the sacrifice of the Mass, on the side of the celebrant, as if she were, so to speak, co-celebrating or even consecrating together with the priest. On the other hand, it would also not be entirely correct to situate her in the church, kneeling among those who are participating in the Mass. Mary is the mother of the whole Church—she is the mother both of the Church's priests and of her lay people. The Mass is Christ's sacrifice on the Cross, insofar as the Church identifies herself with this. What the Mass postulates is the sacrifice of the Cross, accomplished by Christ himself and co-accomplished in a maternal manner by Mary. On this premise, it is possible to speak of the share of the priest and that of the faithful in the Mass as an ecclesiastical sacramental sacrifice of the Cross. By the Cross Mary is the personified or "typical" community of faith and kneels as a faithful participant during the sacrifice of the High Priest. The priesthood is, however, one of the fruits of Christ's redemption in which Mary was involved through her most intimate maternal communion. This is what we mean when we say that Mary is outside the act of consecration, but that her universal and maternal influence embraces both the priest's act of consecration and the co-sacrifice and active participation of the faithful laity.

Mary, then, is on the one hand on the side of the High Priest, Jesus, and on the other on our side—on the side of redeemed humanity. It was this fact which caused the Church to hesitate for so long before expressing an opinion concerning Mary's "priesthood." In 1907 St. Pius X granted indulgences to those who used the pious ejaculation "Mary, Virgin and Priestess, pray for us." In 1917, however, the Church forbade the printing and distribution of holy pictures showing Mary in priestly vestments and finally condemned, in 1927, the devotion to the so-called priesthood of Mary. Mary's mediatorship is not of a priestly kind, and for this reason also not of a sacramental kind. As our mother, she is also the mother of the priesthood. St. Bonaventure expressed it in this way: "In the tabernacle of Mary's virgin womb . . . Christ clothed himself in his priestly vestments so that he might appear as our *pontifex*,"[10] and pseudo-Anselm thus: "It was from thee, Mary, that our High Priest took the host of his body, the host which he offered up on the altar of the Cross for the salvation of the whole world."[11] Mary is the mother of the sacrificing priest and of the oblation and those who receive it. She is the mother of the redemption which was brought by Christ alone. She translates into maternal terms everything that Christ alone, God in humanity, is able to do and in fact does both in our objective redemption and in the subjective redemption which is conveyed to us through the medium of sacramental and priestly acts. She lives in communion with her Son's redemptive activity, joined to him in motherly love. Even though she is certainly outside the hierarchical Church and is fully a member of the community

[10] *Sermo de B.V.M. de Annuntiatione IV.*
[11] *Oratio LV,* al. 54 (*PL,* 158, col. 962).

of the Church, she is nonetheless in the Church, the mother both of the ordinary believer and of the hierarchy. She is the mother in the Church both in the Church's teaching authority and in her governing authority and pastoral office, because she occupies an eminent position in the work of redemption which the hierarchical Church must draw on.

We have thus been able to establish new evidence, in the sacramental life of the Church, to found the exceptional function which we attributed previously to Mary in the divine plan of salvation. Mary has a maternal and all-embracing share both in the historical accomplishment of the redemption of all mankind brought about by the original, primordial sacrament, Christ, and in the separate "subjective redemption" and sanctification of all men brought about by the individual sacraments. As the mother of our "objective redemption" (i.e., Christ), Mary is the mother of all men and of all peoples, even *before* they come to faith in Christ. When Christian missionaries come to a hitherto unknown missionary territory they find that Mary has already been there for a long time, and that she has already filled the water-pots with water and is only waiting for the priests who will follow her and bring about the miracle of Cana in Christ's name. She is, however, in a special sense the mother of all those who have already been baptized in Christ—in such cases, objective redemption has become a personal rebirth. The feelings which a mother has for her child before its birth are, of course, quite different from her feelings for it after it has been born. The mother of all peoples is in a very special sense the mother of all those Christians whose life is derived from the sacraments of the Church.

PART TWO

Our Vital Response
to Mary Our Mother

4

THE VENERATION OF MARY

In Part One of this book I have given a broad outline of the place of Mary in the plan of salvation. This plan of salvation implies a divine activity which demands an active response on the part of man, and in addition makes this human response possible. The question which immediately presents itself, in the context of Mary's special and indeed exceptional function in the divine plan of salvation, is, of course, What place must she occupy in our conscious Christian experience, our explicitly experienced life as Christians? What ought our response to be, what specifically religious form ought it to take, how should we respond to the religious reality of Mary, the Mother of the Redeemer and of the Redemption?

THE VENERATION OF THE SAINTS

Our veneration of the saints is an act of faith, hope and charity. Considered as a synthetic experience of the three theological virtues, it is identical with the Christian love of God. The Communion of Saints, bound together by Christ and with Mary as the maternal factor, forms the basis of all veneration of the saints. The unity of this community of grace is, in turn, based on the God-man, Christ, who is, by vocation, the head of the human race and contains within himself the concrete, supernatural vocation or life-destiny and offers this to us through his incarnation. Christ, as the head of the human race united in its call to salvation, possesses the fullness of grace. He is the fountain-head, the absolute source, of grace (*gratia*

capitis),[1] for he *is* grace. This divine life in Christ, conveyed to
men, is what constitutes the unity of the Communion of Saints. All
holiness, then, even Mary's holiness, is purely a participation in
Christ's holiness. Christ's holiness is in no way enhanced by our
holiness. The holiness of Christ, together with that of Mary and the
whole of the Mystical Body, is in no way greater than the holiness
of Christ alone.[2] From this we may conclude that our explicit experience of Christ is at the same time also an implicit worship of
the saints and that, conversely, our explicit veneration of the saints
is, so to speak, an explication of our experience of Christ. The life
of grace certainly contains within itself an element which enables
the community to be built up. The unity existing between all those
who are informed by grace and the influence which all those who
receive grace have upon each other are always objectively present,
even when this interrelationship is not obviously present, in thought,
feelings or explicit will.

Nevertheless, it is in accordance with the dynamic of any life of
grace which is growing that this mutual relationship should become
an explicitly experienced reality. Christian charity is the realization
of our sanctified condition. Sanctifying grace unites all men and,
when experienced personally, its essential unity is brotherly love.
Veneration of the saints is, on the one hand, one of the most important fruits of brotherly love. On the other hand, the help which
the saints give us is essentially connected with their glorious state
of grace. Just as our love of Christ cannot be separated from our
fraternal love, so it would be wrong to regard veneration of the
saints as superfluous to Christian worship, or as an optional salutary
practice. In this sense, worship of the saints, considered as an aspect
of general worship rather than as a particular devotional practice,
is a duty for every Christian. The complete Christ whom we wor-

---

[1] See especially *ST*, III, q. 7, a. 11.

[2] "In Christo autem bonum spirituale non est particulatum, sed est
totaliter et integrum; unde ipsum est totum Ecclesiae bonum, nec est aliquid
maius *Ipse et alii quam* Ipse solus." (St. Thomas, *In IV Sent.*, d. 49, q. 4, a.
3, ad 4.)

ship is Christ together with the full flowering of all his saints. Christ is the "Crown of All the Saints," as we pray on All Saints' Day. As we have already seen, the holiness of the blessed is no more than a sharing in Christ or a gift of Christ, in the sense that, in their free and personal acceptance of grace, they occupy an irreplaceable position in the divine dispensation of grace. Because of this, all the saints have an essential significance within the plan of salvation for the whole community of grace. All explicit experience of Christ is inevitably bound to develop into an explicit worship of the saints.

True religion is not a neo-Platonic repentance and conversion to God *alone*. We meet God himself, a God who is in love with the world, in the very heart of every religious act. The place which a chosen creature occupies in God's love determines the degree of precedence in which this particular being ought to be regarded in our religious lives.

THE DISTINCTIVE QUALITY
OF THE VENERATION OF MARY

If a direct experience of Christ is at the same time an implicit veneration of the saints, it is bound to follow that this is also, in a special sense, an implicit devotion to Mary, by virtue of her special and unique holiness. Because of this, it should not be difficult to understand how it was possible for St. Paul, for example, and the saints living during the first centuries of Christianity not to show any marked devotion to Mary of the kind with which we are familiar now. An explicit devotion to Mary presupposes, at least in part, the dogmatic development of the Marian mystery, although the more confused appreciation of Mary prevalent during the early Christian period certainly provided the latent force which facilitated the later development of Marian dogma and enabled it eventually to flourish. This indicates quite clearly that devotion to Mary, explicit to a greater or lesser extent, is an essential expression of Christian life. It also indicates that, even though every Christian life is objectively and fundamentally influenced by Mary, it is at the same time possible for certain saints to lead Christian lives in widely differing circumstances, without an explicit devotion to Mary playing a particularly important part. It is, of course, not so much a question of the extent to which we express or explicitly emphasize our devotion to Mary or not, as the case may be. Far more important is the ardour with which we live out our lives as Christians, in faith, hope and charity, and thus in fact follow Mary, who in turn registers the degree of our true Marial experience.

We should, however, not lose sight of the very special quality of the veneration of Mary. Worship of Mary is not a devotion, like that to St. Anthony or St. Apollonia. The Marian cult is on a completely different level, by reason of the exceptional place which the Mother of God occupies in the divine dispensation of grace and thus in the lives of all human beings.

The fact that there are Marian dogmas, and no dogmas at all concerning St. Anthony, for example, indicates clearly that Christian veneration of Mary is not simply different in degree from all other devotions, but is radically superior to them. Our worship of Mary is on a higher level than our general worship of the saints. The existence of dogmas concerning Mary points to the fact that Mary, as a person, belongs essentially to the reality of revelation. Every dogma has a concrete significance within the plan of salvation and has an intimate relationship with the very core of our religious attitude. Dogma forms one single whole, and the whole of dogma is echoed in each separate dogmatic detail. The Christian's experience of Mary is thus, at the same time, a religious experience of the totality of faith. It is, in other words, an experience of the whole of Christian life, viewed from one definite dogmatic perspective.

Dogma is a definite call made by God to men. For us, this means that we are in a special way addressed by God's love and that this divine love which appeals to us through dogma demands our attention and a response on our part. The dogmatic figure which is the Mother of God thus implies a divine appeal to devotion to Mary, a call which comes to us from the very heart of the Redemption itself. For this reason, veneration of Mary is firmly embedded in the Christian religion, and its neglect inevitably leads to a disfigurement of Christian life.

Let us assume, on the basis of what has been discussed in the earlier part of this book, that the following premises are accepted. Firstly, our acceptance of and co-operation in the mystery of Christ implies our personal subjective redemption. Secondly, our personal co-operation in the spread of the Kingdom of God rests on our belief in and understanding of the reality of what the mystery of Christ implies for us and for all men. Thirdly, and as a result of this, we come to accept, in faith and understanding, that Mary—as a singular and exceptional but nonetheless essential and real structural principle—forms an integral part of the redeeming mystery of Christ, that is to say, as the mother of the God-man and, by virtue of her divine motherhood, at the same time as our mother. If the foregoing is accepted, then we are bound, in the mature, adult form of our subjective redemption—and consequently in our mature apostolic activity in the service of God's kingdom as well—to experience Mary's objective and universal relationship with each individual Christian life and come explicitly and consciously under its influence. Our life of prayer will only gain in intensity and effectiveness so long as our prayers objectively form part of the lifelong prayer of Mary's *fiat,* and thus ascend to the Father through the Son—in other words, so long as we explicitly and consciously unite our prayers to the prayer of Mary, the "Suppliant Omnipotence."

It would be, as Pope Pius XII pointed out in his encyclical *Fulgens Corona,* quite wrong to claim, on a basis of the notion that Mary's honour and glory are entirely derived from the redeeming Christ, that all explicit worship of the Virgin is merely optional. It is, of course, true that we may not attribute any single aspect, feature or characteristic to Mary by which she, in her real irreplaceable quality, might be regarded as *adding to* the redemption brought by Christ alone. We have already pointed out that she explicates, in her maternal quality, one aspect of Christ's redemption which could not be made explicit by Christ himself. For this reason, Mary's explication of God's maternal redeeming love is an absolutely irreplaceable element in the divine plan of salvation. It is therefore possible for us to say that Mary adds to Christ's redemption only insofar as she makes it more explicit in some way. One could say that hers is an addition by means of pure explication, of a kind which could not occur in the case of the Redeemer himself.

There is a certain similarity between Mary's case and the saving need of explicit membership in the Church. The Church owes everything she possesses to Christ, her head. Nothing of what the Church is able to give to her members can be added to that which Christ himself gives. Yet, as Pius XII says in his encyclical *Mystici Corporis,* it is only when man is not simply in good faith but is also ready to become a member, in the explicit sense, of the Church community, that one can speak of mature Christianity. Full Christian life can only be Church life. In the same way, the full Christian life must also be essentially Marian life, as an irreplaceable function has been assigned to Mary within the Christian order of salvation. It is possible to compare Mary, in this instance, to God's creation, which is a pure gift, adding nothing to God and making him in no way richer. All the same, God's creation does possess an irreplaceable value and importance of its own, and it is both possible and permissible for us to enter into and enjoy this created world. We may love the creatures of God's creation and respect their individual importance for what they are in themselves. In so doing, however, we should not forget that they are pure gifts of God which cannot in any way add to his glory. At the level of the Redemption, Mary is Christ's most beautiful creation. She has her own individual and irreplaceable function to fulfil within the plan of salvation, but this in no way adds to Christ's redemptive work. At the level of the created world we should not, as it were, behave as if creatures did not exist, in the sophistic fallacy that they add nothing new to God's total importance. In precisely the same way, we should not "pretend," at the level of our religious life of grace, that Mary does not play an essential part in the Christian life, as a wrong

inference from the premise that she can in no way add, in the real
sense, to the redemption brought by Christ alone.

An explicit veneration of Mary is a vitally necessary condition
for the full flowering and normal adult maturity of Christian life.
Its distinctive quality is, moreover, based on the objective fact of
God's having geared the mystery of Mary—as a singular but real
structural principle—to the redemptive mystery of Christ and hence
to the essential mystery of our religious life. This implies that a task
of great importance for all men was assigned by God to Mary in
connection with the vocation of mankind given to us in the person
of Christ. Her unique place within the plan of salvation is an appeal
made by God to all men. We are bound, in faith and love, to recognize this call and to give our assent to it, because we must, in our
constantly growing consciousness of faith, enter into the scheme of
salvation in accordance with God's objective will.

The other aspect of this divine appeal or vocation implies that
we should consciously realize, in faith and loving dedication, Mary's
special relationship to us all, in our Christian lives. This awareness
should consequently lead us to turn this objective and vital relationship into an effective motivating force for the increase of our
personal holiness and the furtherance of our external apostolate. It
is a remarkable fact that, since the Church has become more and
more fully and explicitly conscious of the exceptional function of
the Blessed Virgin in the course of her history, the lives of her
great saints have been marked by a special devotion to Mary. This
fact clearly bears out the objective existence of an essential link
between the veneration of Mary and the *mature* Christian life. That
God, who is intimately acquainted with the human heart—and "the
heart of humanity is the human heart of the God-man"—should
provide a mother for Jesus and for us as an essential element in
his scheme of grace, is undoubtedly a sign of his boundless and
deep loving solicitude for us. The Christian who is explicitly aware
of the part allocated to Mary in God's plan of salvation cannot
afford to neglect the Blessed Virgin in his explicit life of faith. If
he does so, he will inevitably do a grave injustice to his divine voca-

tion, misinterpret the objective and basic features of the Christian way of life and remain deaf to God's loving care. He will, moreover, fail to be fervently committed to faith, and will not throw himself into the great tide which would carry him along towards the full maturity of personal holiness. That is why preachers—and all those who would bear witness to the Christian faith—have the duty to proclaim the full and glorious reality of the mystery of Mary, since this mystery, this dogma, lies at the very heart of the Christian religion.

It is, however, most important that all those entrusted with this duty should be very discreet in their propagation of any one particular form of Marian devotion. In any discussion of the various types of Marian devotion, it is essential to bear in mind that no one particular practice may be considered as the only means of achieving sanctity, and that any fanatical practice is bound to be pernicious and result in false devotion to Mary. In a large family all the children revere their mother, and each child shows its veneration in its own way. Various clearly defined *types* of reverence or veneration may come into existence as the result of a merging of certain features and particular emphases. No one individual type can ever claim a monopoly for itself. It is possible for certain types to have demonstrated their fruitfulness and thus to have become firmly established in the course of the Church's life. Many practices of this kind have, of course, been officially encouraged by the Church herself. But even in such cases we are obliged to distinguish between the essential core of a special devotion of this type and the form and language in which it is expressed. This is generally restricted to a particular period of history and may well, with the gradual development of the spiritual life, become a decided obstacle to worship and spiritual progress. Many excellent devotions are frequently deprived of their potency and efficacy because they are still presented in our day and age in a language and terminology which were perfectly intelligible and acceptable to people in the past, but nowadays tend to go very much against the grain. It ought to be possible for us to keep hold of the essential core of a particular devotion which was propagated in the first place, for example, by a saint, but at the same time to have the courage to strip off and discard its out-of-date husk. Such action would by no means be disloyal, and would result only in good, as far as the spread of these older devotions is concerned.

Let us take one example of antiquated terminology in this context, the phrase "slave of Mary." It is quite obvious, both from the cultural and from the *religious* point of view, that this term cannot hope to make a favourable impact or produce the right effect nowadays. In the past this phrase may well have concealed a deep religious reality. Today it is absolutely unacceptable, and its use can only lead to total misunderstanding. The reader should not impute pride to this condemnation—the very opposite is true. It is simply that the present-day Christian is incapable of embodying in his life the idea of total loving surrender if this is presented to him in the form of "loving slavery." The greatest tribute which could be paid to St. Louis Grignion de Montfort would be to free his profound vision from its now out-of-date terminology, which today hinders rather than promotes devotion to the Blessed Virgin.

This, of course, applies to the whole of Christian life. As a result of such a separation of the wheat from the chaff, we may very often discover that a particular devotion—and this is certainly true of the prayer of the Rosary—is fundamentally nothing more nor less than a specially arranged synthesis of Marian devotions with a truly trinitarian and Christological orientation. And it is precisely this aspect of any genuine devotion to Mary which is essential and irreplaceable.

THE DANGER OF "MARIANISM"

To our plea for an explicit worship of Mary as a necessary condition for the mature Christian life there must be added a warning of the danger inherent in popular devotions to Mary. It sometimes happens that the emphasis is subtly shifted in such popular manifestations of Marian worship. This shift of emphasis is often quite spontaneous; occasionally it can be traced to the activity of certain organizations which have placed themselves under the protection of Mary. It is, however, most important to remember that Mary can only be understood when seen in the perspective of Christ and that it is an error to view Christ from the perspective of Mary. If we accept that both an explicit experience of Christ and an explicit worship of Mary form part of the mature Christian life, then it follows that a Marian life in which this experience of Christ remains more or less implicit must always be an immature form of Christianity. Indeed, it is possible to go further, and say that such a life will be even less mature than a Christian life in which devotion to Mary is merely implicit. This implication of an experience of Christ in an explicit devotion to Mary constitutes what we may call "Marianism." Christ is the gleaming jewel contained in the casket which is Mary. If we fail to encounter Christ, directly and explicitly, at the very centre of this casket, we are bound to misunderstand Mary's true greatness—the unfathomable mystery of her reception of Christ and her longing for the only Mediator.

Our way to Christ is through Mary. This fact is, however, often falsely interpreted. One of the commonest errors is to think that the man Jesus is rather remote from us and that the gulf is, as it were, bridged by Mary. To regard Mary in this way as the link between ourselves and a distant Christ is totally to misconstrue the deepest meaning of the Incarnation—the fact that Christ became our fellow, a man like us. This in turn inevitably leads to a fundamental falsification of the central Christian vision of life—the significance for us of Christ's sacred *humanity* as the divine organ instituted by God for our salvation. Christ was born of Mary. Because of this, he is emphatically one of us. He was brought *close to us* by Mary. The relationship between Christ and ourselves is, therefore, direct. There can be no intervening agency. He alone is the Mediator between God and mankind, and this is so by virtue of the fact that he was born, as the God-man, of Mary. Everything comes to us from Christ.

He offers his great gift of redemption to us, however, in a special form. It is realized in a sublime and universal form, for our benefit, in Mary, who accepted Christ's gift in the most sublime manner, with the result that her *fiat* takes precedence over ours and that our *fiat* is involved in hers. Together with Mary, and under her influence, we encounter Christ the man directly. He in turn leads us to the Father. In this sense it is better to think of Christ as giving Mary to us as our mother, rather than of Mary as giving us Christ —"Behold thy mother." He freely chose his mother and ours for himself and for all of us—"Elegit eam Deus et praeelegit eam."

In another sense, however—that of her conception of Christ and her passing him on—Mary can be thought of as giving Christ to us. It is in this sense that the meaning of the phrase "through Mary to Christ," emphasized in various papal documents, may be understood at its deepest level. Mary is, by definition, the *kecharitomene* —the one who has "received *charis*" (Luke 1. 28), that is, the one who has "found grace with God" (Luke 1. 30). This was the title by which the angel addressed her in the Message. Joined to her, we too find grace with God. She is not a link between God and ourselves, but the one womb which gives birth to us as Christ's brothers. She is the casket in which our direct encounter with Christ takes place.

If we gear our response to grace and thus our supplication to Christ to Mary's *fiat,* which includes every prayer of supplication, our prayer will always be heard. It is possible for us to penetrate, in faith and love, more deeply into the mystery of Christ's redemption and for Mary's child, Christ, to grow within us, since Mary is "suppliant omnipotence," suppliant, because she is purely receptive. Mary can teach us how to be Christian in our lives. To live in unity with Mary is essentially and in the purest sense a Christocentric life, and for this reason it is impossible for any child of Mary to "go astray." The Christian never prays alone. The entire communion of saints prays with him, and this community which prays is itself included in the universal power of supplication of the mother of the Mystical Body.

A devotion to Mary does not, however, acquit us from any part of our religious involvement with Christ. We should not for one moment imagine that our veneration for Mary is likely to make it easier for us to lead *vicariously* Christian lives, by substituting Mary for ourselves. Sometimes we are inclined to put it in this way: as far as our lives as Christians are concerned we are just hopeless bunglers, doomed to make a mess of everything. This is, in a sense, quite true! But, we go on to think, if we let Mary do our praying and our work for us, everything will be all right. Of course, if by this we mean that we are striving to identify ourselves so completely with Mary's prayer and work that we deepen our own faith and intensify our own love, then everything will indeed be all right. But in this case the question of substituting Mary for ourselves does not arise. If, on the other hand, we mean that we are using Mary in this instance as a substitute for our own shortcomings, and consequently do not deepen our own faith, strengthen our hope in Christ's saving power and intensify our Christian love by means of this explicit Marian devotion, then in my opinion the practice is bound to be unjustified and ineffectual. We grow in holiness as God penetrates more and more deeply into our souls. This divine penetration demands a personal and free commitment in the existential religious sense on our part, and we are able to achieve this together with Mary and in the power of her love. We can never accomplish it by trying to enlist the services of Mary to make up for our essential shortcomings and our real failure to surrender totally in faith, for it is only through this total submission that what is impossible to man may become possible to God.

We should also be far more careful in our use of human analogies in this respect if we are to remain fully aware of the specifically Marian function which the Mother of God fulfils in the Christian order of redemption. An example of this is the idea of the so-called "French School," that Mary again and again tempers God's—and Christ's—justice and that she is able at the last moment to hold back Christ's arm raised in punishment. This image, of course, had an important part to play in the case of the visionaries of La Salette. It cannot be denied that it is a very striking way of illustrating Mary's intervention through the power of supplication, but it certainly does nothing to promote a true appreciation of the real saving function of *Christ* himself. Mary's mercy is entirely derived from the compassion of Christ, the God-man, who showed a superabundance of compassion to her as the firstfruit of the Redemption. Mary displays, in her person, the *maternal* aspect of this divine mercy. It is, of course, possible to "contrast" Mary's maternal quality with God's mercy, but it is never permissible to regard her maternal intervention as a kind of counterbalance to Christ's divine justice, even though her intervention is really effective. We should, on the other hand, bear in mind in this context that we can often come to a closer understanding of the divine reality simply by talking on the human level about God and his relationship with mankind than by the more precise process of theological discussion!

POPULAR DEVOTION TO MARY

An Argument for the "Fringe Manifestations" in the Religious Life of the People

God is the Father of mercy and, as such, he shows boundless mercy towards us in our errors. He can always see beyond the almost superstitious and sometimes disturbing credulity of certain practices and expressions of popular devotion and perceive the good intentions of his poor, inadequate creatures, who are not able to express, in the right words and in fitting actions, their deep longing for God which, until they are finally capable of surrendering unconditionally to God, must inevitably result in restlessness in their lives.

The candle, left quietly burning, in timid humility, in front of the statue of Mary after the pilgrim has gone away from the shrine, can be seen as a symbol of the Christian's impotence. He leaves this candle behind because he is not yet fully capable of surrendering completely in faith to God's dispensation, of letting his heart melt away in the glow of this total submission. The material creation—the candle—is more responsive to God's touch and more readily fashioned than the living heart of man, which is less willing to let itself be trimmed and pruned by the heavenly Lord of the Vineyard. And so the Christian, in his human longing, lights the willing candle as a tangible supplication to God. By means of the intercession of the Mother of God, he hopes to inflame his capricious human heart and his obdurate human will and make them both kneel in homage. The candle, still burning quietly before the statue of Mary while the pilgrim joins the crowd haggling noisily over the high prices of the *souvenirs de Lourdes,* is a visible demonstration of the deep longing which is always present in the human heart and which, though hidden and perhaps seldom expressed, will live on long after the candle has burnt out its ephemeral existence.

The candle is not a lie. Nor is the endless movement of the pilgrims round the shrine of Mary a lie. They are an evocative image of the restless, wandering human heart which cannot find repose until, tired of wandering, it finally comes to rest close to God who touched this earth in Mary. The journey which our heart cannot or will not make has thus to be undertaken by the body, in an endlessly repeated gesture, an impotent effort to contradict the unwillingness of our heart. We should therefore not be too rash in passing judgment. Rather we should try to fashion these external images into a genuine religious internal experience.

There are, then, numerous "fringe manifestations" in Marian life, and these can be understood if they are viewed in the light of the symbolism which is so closely interwoven with the lives of men who attain to invisible realities by means of what is visible. These expressions are essentially prototypes among the various manifestations of popular religious life, and are as old as the human race itself. No amount of intellectualism will ever succeed in eradicating them from the religious life of the people. Man has need of such props. He feels the need to stroke with his hand the rock where the Mother of God appeared. It is important for him to be able to climb, on his knees or even crawling, up the steps of the Stations of the Cross. Religion is not simply a question of the interior life. It is not a purely rational matter. Any claim that religion is exclusively rational is contradicted by Bernadette's crawling over the ground and swallowing grass and mud—and doing this on the instigation of the "Lady" who appeared to her. These manifestations are bound to make us think of the faith of Abraham—a belief and trust in God despite all human evidence to the contrary. Man has to create a setting for his religious life in this world, a visible environment in which he can live on intimate terms and at the human level with the transcendent.

There is, of course, a danger in all this. The moment that religion is really imprisoned in earthly reality, the moment that the soul of religion disappears from the universally human symbolic activity, then the power of the sacred symbolism to uplift man is lost. Whenever this happens, nothing but soulless ritualism remains, and religion is reduced to mere folklore.

On the other hand, however, religion can never exist as a distinct and separate department in human life. It is intricately bound up with the whole of the life of the community, and genuine folklore has its rightful place here. No one who has a genuine human sympathy for his fellows need be annoyed or scandalized by the fact that pilgrimages are frequently accompanied by various manifestations of folklore. It is especially important for intellectuals to guard against a too critical attitude in this matter. They are, after all, rarely asked to take an enthusiastic part in this aspect of the religious life of the ordinary people! What they must try to do, however, is to develop a true understanding of such all-too-human fringe manifestations, for it is certain that any successful attempt to banish all this from religious life by a cold, rational appeal to return to "authentic" religious practice would inevitably result in the death of popular devotion and possibly, too, in the death of people's religious life itself.

On the other hand, however, it is important for us not to ignore one fundamental aspect of the teaching of all religions, and especially of that of the Old Testament. From time to time the Prophets had to make their voices heard, and make the people conscious of the need to intensify their interior religious life. If a Christian people is inattentive to this prophetic call its worship of the Lord will eventually become mere lip-service.

When the people of Ephesus, full of enthusiasm for their pagan religion, were provoked, they cried incessantly: "Great is Diana of the Ephesians!" (Artemis, the Greek goddess). The sarcastic comment of the clerk who addressed the crowd was: "That may well be so. I have already heard more than enough about the greatness of your goddess" (see Acts 19. 28, 34–6). A few centuries later, however, the same enthusiasm filled the streets of Ephesus, but by then it was in honour of the Mother of God. The religious enthusiasm of the ordinary people is not wrong. Everything depends on the object of this enthusiasm and its orientation.

Every renewed spiritualization is bound to manifest itself in the life of the people in a renewed externalization, and anyone who successfully attacks the human incarnations of such spiritual forms will at the same time kill the inner human spirit. Nevertheless, these fringe manifestations must always be subjected to dogmatic enlightenment. Because of their almost fanatical power in the human life of the people, popular devotions have everything to gain from being continually purified of the various elements which all too quickly become almost inextricably interwoven with the authentic human manifestations of genuine Christian life. Nowadays this tends to happen especially in connection with the popular craving for miraculous events. This is particularly noticeable in the extreme popular interest in the various apparitions of Mary. It is therefore with reference to these particular facts that such popular manifestations should come under the special guidance of theological enlightenment.

The Apparitions and Their Place in the Religious Life of the People

There can be little doubt that the repeated apparitions of Mary in our times which have already been given ecclesiastical approval

—the most notable of these being the apparitions made to Catherine Labouré (1830), at La Salette (1846),[3] at Lourdes (1858), at Pontmain (1871), at Fatima (1917), at Beauraing (1932) and at Banneux (1933)—indicate that God is aware that we are going through especially difficult times and that Mary, the mother of religious mankind, manifests her maternal solicitude in a special way.

It often happens, however, that these extraordinary interventions are not appreciated at their true value in sermons and at the devotional level. Sometimes they are given an exaggerated value, sometimes they are underestimated. For this reason, it is of some importance to examine the Church's attitude towards such extraordinary facts of Christianity, set this out schematically and attempt to establish the exact place of these phenomena within the dogmatically enlightened Marian life.

Christianity is God's love of man made visible in the history of the world. The Old Testament prepared the way for this, it was accomplished in Christ and it was sacramentally perpetuated in the Church. This revelation of God's plan to save mankind was brought to a close on the death of the last apostolic witness of Christ. This means that before his public revelation had come to a close, God was still able to intervene in human history in such a way that mankind's situation with regard to God could still be radically changed. Even after his revelation had come to a close, however, God continued to intervene in history, not to inaugurate a new order of salvation, but to focus attention on the historical fact of Christ. With Christ, the "fullness of time" really dawned, and, as we have already seen, Mary has an essential and irreplaceable function to fulfil within this Christian establishment of a permanent way of life.

From that time forward, there were no new revelations which were essential to man's salvation. We are able to encounter

---

[3] It should not be forgotten, however, that the Church has repeatedly forbidden the spread of the prophecies of La Salette. (*AAS* [1915], vol. 7, p. 594, and 1923, vol. 15, pp. 287–8.)

Christ's sacred humanity by means of the Church's faith and her sacraments. Since these bring Christ's "objective redemption" to us in a sacramental manner, all that we have to do is to enter both into the living faith of the Church and into her sacraments in order to be bathed by redemption and at the same time become *personally* redeemed. In the sacramental Church, then, everything that is necessary for our sanctification is present in abundance. The Church's life of faith is regulated in all this exclusively by the revelation-in-reality and revelation-in-word, which is entrusted to the Church as a living treasury of faith. It can, therefore, never be regulated by private revelations. This applies both to the revelations of the Sacred Heart which were made after God's public revelation had come to a close[4] and to those of Mary, however authentic these may be, since they do not in any sense form *structural principles* of the Church instituted for man's salvation.

But this, of course, is only one aspect of the question. In addition to the hierarchical element—the Church's governing authority and her teaching and pastoral offices, all of which are established in the sacramental Church as a community of faith—there is also a prophetic, charismatic element in the Church. The Holy Ghost, as the soul of the Church, penetrates the entire community of faith. It does not simply enter the community from above, that is to say, in and through its guidance of the hierarchy. It also acts *from within,* with the result that its influence is perceptible even in the most insignificant members of the community of faith. In this way it is possible for the Holy Ghost to bypass the hierarchy and inwardly stimulate any faithful member of the Church, inspiring him to such an extent that what he becomes or does will be a blessing for the whole Church. In the Church everything is guided from above—in other words, the Church is hierarchically guided. But all that is concentrated in the ecclesiastical hierarchy as a living ministry of Christ in an official manner—that is, in a

---

[4] Christ's apparitions after his resurrection and before his ascension still form part of the *mysteria carnis Christi,* that is to say, they form part of Christ's mission on earth, which came to an end only with the Ascension.

manner pertaining to office in the Church—can at the same time exist in a non-official manner in the whole of the Church community, which is, in the non-official sense, "both priestly and royal and prophetic and charismatic." Thus it may happen that, under the impulse of the Holy Ghost and from the very heart of the non-hierarchical community, initiatives may arise which may be of great importance for the whole of the Church's life and which may later be sanctioned in one way or another by the hierarchical Church. In this sense the Church still lives, as did the primitive Church, from her office and from her charism, even though it is possible for the manner in which this charism reveals itself to vary considerably throughout the course of history.

In our opinion the various authentic apparitions of Mary really belong to this prophetic or charismatic element of the Church's life. They are, of course, known as private revelations, as opposed to the public revelation of Christ. Public revelation is directly entrusted to the hierarchical Church, and its content includes the vital dogmatic and moral principles of Christian religious life. The Church is profoundly aware of her direct responsibility in this connection and positively vouches for it. Private revelations are external to the constitution of the Church. They do not form part of it in the same way as does public revelation. They do not, in their doctrinal content, incorporate any elements which are capable of enlarging or extending the scope of public revelation. No new dogma or law is ever proclaimed in them. As far as the constitutional aspect of the Church's life is concerned, these private revelations are merely marginal, secondary phenomena, existing side by side with and in the perspective of the life of grace of the saving community. They are not in any sense calculated to clarify doctrinal points arising from public revelation, and should therefore never be used to settle questions brought up in theological discussion. There are other, vital organs of the Church already in existence which can be used precisely for this purpose.

On the other hand, it would be equally wrong to claim that God, who takes a direct hand in all private revelations, even though he makes use of human psychology in all its subtle depths, wished to communicate quite unimportant things to us or to tell us something that we ought to know already.[5] We may, and indeed are bound to, state *a priori* that private revelations and apparitions of this kind are acts of loving solicitude on the part of God and our heavenly mother. They are little tokens of love from the God who loves us and who has already demonstrated his love for us "unto death," thus in such superabundance that these little extra signs of love really seem to be of no account. Yet this is, of course, not true. These little signs are of importance. Even though God's love may be absolute beauty and even though Mary may be the *Mater Pulchrae Dilectionis* who always gives far more than is strictly necessary, there is a still deeper significance contained in these private revelations.

If we wish to avoid a misunderstanding of the essential meaning of public revelation on the one hand, and the suggestion on the other that private revelations are useless and superfluous, then there is only one possible formulation of the phenomenon of private revelation open to us. In private revelations the dogmatic and moral content of faith is confronted with present-day situations, in which it is "necessary" for God, in his love, to make his concrete will known, in an exceptional and charismatic manner, to men who are, by reason of their very humanity, so firmly tied to the visible and tangible manifestations of the invisible realities of life. In this way private revelations are intimately connected with the guidance of our human actions, though not with the dogma or the official pronouncements of the whole Church. There is always, in the concrete circumstances of our lives, an incalculable, even an ambiguous element which leaves us the choice of several different courses of action. This is especially so, of course, in times of spiritual need. The Church's hierarchy can always help us to choose the right path, but at the same time there is always the charismatic,

[5] In connection with this point, see also K. Rahner, *Visionen und Prophezeiungen,* Innsbruck (1953); J. H. Nicolas, "La Foi et les signes," in *VS,* 1953, *Suppl.* pp. 121–64.

prophetic element in the Church, and it is always possible for the Holy Ghost to inspire us, either as individuals or as a group, to action through this element. In all cases, however, the Church is subject to the guidance of the Holy Ghost, although the various apparitions and private revelations which we have been discussing form an exceptional, yet real element of charismatic inspiration.

In this sense they are of the same order as the Church's concrete life, though they do not form a constituent part of the Church. They are, therefore, by no means so "marginal" as we may at first be inclined to think, and it is of some importance to distinguish between the ways in which these private revelations and apparitions take place; in contrast to the many relatively obscure instances of the appearance of the prophetic element in the life of the Church, the charismatic element is frequently revealed, in the case of an individual believer, in a most striking psychological manner.

It is, of course, true that the apparition as such *directly* affects only the privileged person. As in the case of every charismatic inspiration, it is always *his* apparition. It often happens that certain elements contained in the apparition are of a strictly personal nature, and sometimes there is an injunction to secrecy. All the same, as charism, every apparition is destined to become a blessing for the life of the Church. This may have a world-wide application. On the other hand, it may be restricted to a particular place, region or nation. Apparitions and private revelations are, therefore, a divine inspiration providing a guide or signpost which will show Christians the path to salvation in a definite spiritual situation and at a definite point of time. When God brought his public revelation to a close he did not cease at that moment to intervene personally in the history of mankind.

Every expression of the charismatic element in the life of the Church is, however, always subject to the control of the hierarchy. We propose, therefore, to indicate, in a brief, schematic outline, some of the main features of the attitude of the Church and of Christians towards the apparitions of Mary. We shall not deal with the psychological or technical aspect of these apparitions in this outline. That is to say, we shall not discuss, for example, whether or not our Lady really appeared in her living body. (In passing, however, it should be noted that this is not an entirely absurd *a priori* claim, at least as far as an apparition of Mary is concerned, in view of the fact that she is already in physical glory. It does, however, pose the question of psychological adaptation between glorified and non-glorified corporeality.) Nor do we propose to discuss whether or not it is only visions of the imagination, made miraculous by God or even brought about in a purely providential manner, which postulate a certain psychological disposition. (The Church permits us to regard such cases in this way, and it cannot be denied that very many of the facts point in this direction.) The main point, however, is firstly that there is always a personal contact with the saint in person (in this case, our Lady), in all authenticated apparitions, and, secondly, that the "form" which the apparition takes—and this may be of a psychological nature—is a "sign" in which this personal contact is implied and inwardly embodied.

(1) In the first place we must insist that this extraordinary charismatic element is always subordinate to the normal moral and religious life of grace which is informed by dogma. For this reason, too, the charismatic element must always remain subordinate to the normal life of grace in the Church's preaching. Apparitions and similar phenomena are able to shock people whose faith is weak and bring them back to the true "sign of God," the God-man Jesus Christ, but they are of absolutely no avail to people whose minds are completely closed. One has only to think in this context of Bruce Marshall's novel, *Father Malachy's Miracle,* although this is, of course, a parody of the situation. For people whose faith is already firm, apparitions are an expression of God's love, which is, in any case, something with which they are already familiar. The convinced believer, then, will regard apparitions as "normal," accept them calmly and thank God and the Blessed Virgin for their loving solicitude in difficult times and try to live more Christian lives.

(2) We do not believe in apparitions with *divine* faith, since apparitions are outside the sphere of revealed saving reality. The divine virtue of faith is exercised only in connection with a supernatural saving reality. This means, then, that even something that is communicated to us by God himself is not necessarily an object worthy of divine faith. Let us take the absurd premise that God, in his living body, should reveal Newton's Binomial Theorem to me. It would nonetheless be impossible for me to believe in this with divine faith, since I should accept this theorem as worthy of belief with a human faith, on a basis of positive motives, evident to me, and never with theological faith. Divine faith always implies a supernatural and religious saving reality. Apparitions and private revelations can, therefore, be accepted only with natural faith, in view of the fact that everything that was necessary to determine the religious task of man with regard to God was provided before God's public revelation was brought to a close. Visionaries are faced with a direct "certainty of experience," which has to be subjected to close critical examination before it can be declared authentic. For us, however, to whom the visionaries communicate their apparitions, it is merely a question of cautious approval, based on natural motives for the acceptance of these apparitions as worthy of belief. In other words, we accept them on the authority of the visionaries themselves, whose worthiness of belief has been subjected to critical investigation. It is, therefore, a question of natural approval, justified both on moral and on rational grounds, of a fact which cannot, after it has been fully investigated, be rationally interpreted as demonic in origin,[6] but, when all the circumstances, and especially the religious circumstances, have been taken into consideration, must be regarded as having originally come from God, whether or not it is naturally explicable in terms of depth-psychology. In this case it will be a miraculous apparition.

[6] It should be noted that the phrase "neither *natural* nor demonic" has been avoided here. Some apparitions are, of course, miraculous, whereas others may be interpreted as natural phenomena, with the result that what emerges from the whole authentic and religious context is that God himself has taken a hand in this natural, psychological phenomenon.

(3) The Church's approbation of an apparition or private revelation is, however, never an infallible proof of its historical truth and authenticity. It is merely an official confirmation of the fact that sufficient evidence has emerged from the investigation to enable us to be cautiously certain in our acceptance of the divine authenticity of the apparition on rational grounds.[7] It would perhaps be more precise to say that it is ultimately only a question of an authoritative opinion concerning our cautious approval. To all intents and purposes, the Church does no more than give her official permission that Mary may be venerated in a special way at the place where the apparition has occurred. Her sanction is a sort of *Nihil Obstat*, by means of which she refrains from concerning herself in a positive sense with the concrete content of the apparition.

(4) There is a good deal of controversy among theologians as to whether an ecclesiastical approbation of this kind actually imposes upon the faithful the obligation to accept, in the human sense, the approved fact on rational grounds.[8] In my opinion the rather negative nature of this approbation would seem to rule out any possibility of an obligation. According to the Acts of the Fifth Provincial Council of Malines, "In the opinion of the Church, it is in no way necessary for all the faithful to believe in these matters. All that the Church declares is that, in her judgment, they are in no way contrary to faith and morals and that there are sufficient indications for their pious and cautious approval by human faith."[9]

[7] See, among other works, *Pascendi*, para. 6 (*Actes de Pie X*, vol. 3, p. 175); also *De Servorum Dei Beatificatione et Canonisatione* of Pope Benedict XIV—a work which is still consulted in cases of canonization: "Sciendum est approbationem istam nihil aliud esse quam permissionem ut edantur [in order to make private revelations public] ad fidelium institutionem et utilitatem post maturum examen; siquidem hisce revelationibus taliter approbatis, licet *non debeatur nec possit* adhiberi assensus fidei catholicae, debetur tamen assensus fidei *humanae* iuxta prudentiae regulas, iuxta quas nempe tales revelationes sunt *probabiles* et *pie credibiles*." (Lib. 2, c. 32, no. 11.)

[8] Yves Congar and Karl Rahner, among others, answer this question in the affirmative.

[9] *Acta et Decreta Concilii Provincialis Mechliniensis Quinti*, Malines (1938), p. 6. The technical formulation of ecclesiastical approbation of this

Respect for and docility to the Church can only be indirectly useful in cases such as these. It would, in other words, be unbecoming to attack the Church's decisions openly once they have been made, and to reject them as having no real critical significance for us. Even after the Church has declared her approval, however, it still remains true that apparitions of this kind can appeal only to our religious critical sense. It is quite reasonable for the faithful, and fully justified on their part, to act on the Church's approval, assuming that the case has previously been subjected to critical investigation. Finally, it should be noted that, because of the "incalculable" factor which is always present in the prophetic and charismatic element in the Church, the ecclesiastical hierarchy is always inclined to be extremely critical rather than lenient in all cases of this type. Lourdes and Fatima both provide striking proof of the Church's attitude towards apparitions.

(5) The Church may permit the building of a basilica, institute a new liturgical feast or give her approval to a new devotion, such as the wearing of a special scapular, the "Miraculous Medal," and so on. In all such cases the private revelation is merely an external inducement, never the Church's real motive. The Church's approval of the building of a basilica does not, moreover, imply *per se* the historical truth of the apparition. We may, therefore, wear the Miraculous Medal to our spiritual benefit, without actually believing in the private revelation granted to Catherine Labouré. The devotion is in itself good, and firmly founded in the sacramental life of the Church.

In approving such practices, the Church generally withdraws from a consideration of the private revelation itself and frequently does not even mention it by name, but only establishes its connection with the doctrinal basis of our faith. In 1846, for example, Pope Pius IX gave his immediate approbation to the wearing of the Scapular of the Passion, without even investigating the authen-

kind is: "Apparitio . . . [est] permissa tamquam pie credenda, fide tamen humana, iuxta piam, uti perhibent, traditionem etiam idoneis testimoniis ac monumentis confirmatam." (*Decreta Authentica Congr. S. Rituum*, Rome [1900], vol. 3, no. 3336, p. 48.)

ticity of the private revelations of Sister Andriveau. The call for the institution of a Feast of the Blessed Sacrament was first made in a private revelation. Urban IV approved the institution of this feast—Corpus Christi—by appealing to the dogma itself. It was only afterwards, in the Bull, that a very brief and vague allusion was made to the private revelation. The desire for a feast of this kind was already firmly established in the living tradition of the Church. The private revelation of this longing was, so to speak, the "prophetic element" in which the desire was most powerfully concentrated. In the same way the Feast of the Sacred Heart of Jesus had been, as it were, expected for a long time before the private revelations of St. Margaret Mary. The same applies to the Feast of the Immaculate Heart of Mary, for which petitions had been received from all quarters well before the apparitions at Fatima. For example, the Eucharistic Congress which met in Lourdes in 1914 sent a petition to Rome asking for the institution of this feast—this was several years before the apparitions at Fatima. This shows how the prophetic, charismatic element of an apparition acted as a "concentration" of an impulse already set in motion in the Church by the Holy Ghost. In 1899 Pope Leo XIII dedicated the world to the Sacred Heart of Jesus. This action was, however, not based on the private revelations granted to Mère Marie du Divin Cœur, but exclusively on dogmatic and theological considerations.

All the above instances serve to show how it is public revelation alone which is the norm. Private revelations do no more than support the Church's public revelation. A characteristic example here is the case of Sister Andriveau. She is reputed to have received a communication, in a private revelation, that a feast of the Passion should be instituted during Easter week. The Church refused to inaugurate this feast, because it did not accord with the joy of Easter! Similarly, the bishop who gave his approval to a certain holy picture representing Mary, which was inspired by a private revelation, caused certain features of the "revealed image" to be modified. This action resulted in many protests. The Holy Office settled the matter in a decree dated 8 September 1904. The decree stated that ecclesiastical approbation of the holy picture in no way implied—"either directly or indirectly"—the historical truth of the private revelation! Even the canonization of visionaries, for example, does not guarantee the historicity of possible apparitions, miracles, stigmata and so on.

The declaration in *Pascendi* is also pertinent here: "Veneration, the object of which is an apparition, may only take place, insofar as it refers to the fact itself and is therefore of relative value, on condition that the fact itself is authentic. Insofar as the cult is absolute, it must always be based on the truth, as this cult is aimed *at the person* of the saint whom the faithful wish to venerate. The same reservations apply also to the veneration of relics."[10] In other words, the veneration of "Our Lady of Scherpenheuvel" (or wherever else it may be) is never absolute, though the veneration of Mary herself is.

What we have to impress upon the faithful, then, is that it is a question of venerating the Mother of God herself, rather than "Our Lady of Lourdes," "Our Lady of Fatima" and so on. What is expressly demanded of us, as Christians, is the veneration of the Mother of God. The veneration of "Fatima," "Lourdes" and so on is always purely optional. It is perfectly possible for us to make a pilgrimage to Scherpenheuvel, for example, in a spirit of deep devotion to Mary, without even "believing" in the miraculous events which in the first place led to Scherpenheuvel's being regarded as a holy place. In any case, who has any real knowledge of these events, as far as the ancient holy places are concerned? In the same way, it should also be remembered that particular devotional practices, even those which have become widespread as a result of private revelations, can never imply an obligation. If they do not happen to "suit" us we need never worry about not practising them, although we should be very careful to avoid developing a sharply critical, and even sceptical attitude towards such popular devotions, resulting in a spiritually superior mentality.

[10] *Pascendi,* in *Acta Sanctae Sedis,* 1907, vol. 11, p. 649.

It sometimes happens that preachers and spiritual directors are guilty, here, of restricting the freedom of the individual conscience.

We are bound, then, to conclude from the foregoing that it is positively wrong to talk more about Fatima in a sermon than about our Lady herself, the Mother of God. Pope Pius XII, who was particularly well informed about Fatima, was always extremely reserved in his attitude towards the subject, although it is common knowledge that Fatima played an indirect part in his special appeal for devotion to Mary, which eventually resulted in the inauguration of the Marian Year in 1954. Even in *Fulgens Corona,* the allusion to the historical instance of Lourdes—now regarded as *the* type in the Church of a place specially favoured by Mary— is very unobtrusive and totally subordinated to the dogma. Some preachers habitually go to great lengths to promulgate the promises made in the apparitions of the Sacred Heart or of Mary, while entirely neglecting the essential dogmas concerning Christ and Mary or else simply bringing these dogmas into their sermons as something subservient to one or other private revelation. This is a practice which can never be justified. In sermons of this kind the true emphasis is totally misplaced and, what is more, they can be particularly scandalizing, as we know from experience, to intellectual laity. We have to proclaim the truth of Christianity, but it must at the same time be the pure Christian truth! To give the laity the impression, in sermons of this kind, that there is something wrong with them, that they are failing in true devotion to Mary, if they do not concern themselves with private revelations and so on, is to go counter to the mind of the Church.

An incident from the life of St. John of the Cross may help to illustrate this point. Arriving at a certain town in Spain, his attention was drawn to *la monja de las llagas*—the "nun with the wounds"—a stigmatic who lived in a convent in the town, under the protection of high-ranking prelates, although the Church had made no official pronouncement concerning the authenticity of her case. St. John was asked to visit this nun. Instead of going to see her, however, he went to look at the sea, in order to praise God for his equally miraculous creation!

This is an example of sane and healthy mysticism, never craving for extraordinary signs and wonders, but always aware that we live and breathe in the enduring miracle of God's maternal goodness. Human psychology is such that we are always open to the "extraordinary" element. This is particularly so in difficult times—we have only to think of the war years. We are, however, too easily inclined to forget that this element may soon become a *substitute* in men's minds for a true, and harder, faith in the unknown. Preachers must, therefore, always be alert to possible excesses in their sermons on Fatima, Lourdes and so on, and preach the Mother of God from the Gospel. At La Salette Mary showed her concern for the harvest which was threatened with destruction. This was a private revelation. Far more important, however, is the lesson given to us in public revelation—Mary's concern, at Cana, for the embarrassment of the guests at the wedding feast: "They have no wine." (John 2. 3.)

If we examine the content of the seven universally acclaimed apparitions of Mary which have taken place in our own times we are bound to see how the ancient treasure of Christianity is simply related in these apparitions to the spiritual needs of our own situation. Mary confirms our sinfulness and the fact of Christ's redemption and urges us to prayer and repentance. The circumstances in which this confirmation takes place, however, all point to the charismatic element of divine inspiration, by means of which God seeks to activate this ancient treasure of Christian life in our own times. We must, of course, always exercise great caution in our attitude towards any revelation, and particularly towards the manner in which it is communicated to us by the visionary. The "content" of a private revelation never exists in isolation. It is, on the contrary, always a living part of the total human psychology of the visionary. It is always *mingled* with other elements which are already present in the visionary's consciousness, and these are bound to *colour* and even to contribute towards an interpretation of the content of the revelation as it is communicated to us.

Moreover, the communication of a private revelation, unlike that of public revelation, is not guaranteed by the charism of inspiration. As the "content" of any apparition is always surrounded by numerous psychological elements and impulses and by many details of human imagination, it would be foolish to try, for example, to construct a theology of hell on the basis of the vision of hell communicated to us by the apparitions of Fatima. Here, of course, we have to do with apparitions made to children. It is particularly important in such cases to take into account the psychology of the child, and the childish tendency, albeit in all good faith, to indulge in flights of imagination. The child-visionaries of Fatima, too, were interrogated by a tribunal of impressive theologians, whose questions—many of them set to catch the children out—must often have perplexed them.

The conclusion which we are bound to draw from the foregoing, then, is that, even when reference is made to apparitions on perfectly justifiable grounds, preachers should always be very discriminating in what they say about the details of these private revelations in their sermons. They should be particularly careful to avoid references to details which tend to stimulate human curiosity. To take a concrete example, they should never deal with questions as to whether there will be a war, or whether the war will end soon. Sermons which appeal in this way to private revelations only serve to draw men's minds away from the essence of religion and to encourage them to look for an alibi in apparitions, instead of helping them to intensify their religious attitude and to commit themselves to the concrete moral tasks involved in Christian living.

Preachers are first and foremost heralds of public revelation and, as such, they should make only the most discreet use of private revelations and apparitions. They might justifiably employ them to exemplify or illustrate a particular point in their sermons on Mary, but they should never base their sermons on them. We cannot grasp the essential significance of a miracle by quietly contemplating the extraordinary event. Rather, we grasp it by vividly recalling the fact that God bears up and supports everything that happens even in the ordinary circumstances of our everyday lives and that Mary, the Mother of God, does not, for one single moment, leave herself without testimony. A miracle is a *tonic* which draws our attention back to the ordinary, daily content of our Christian existence. We may regard a miraculous event as a medicine which is occasionally as necessary to us as the bread which forms the basis of our life, but which is given to us so that we shall later on be able to live by our daily bread. "Rather, blessed are they who hear the word of God and keep it" (Luke 11. 28)—it was with these words that Jesus corrected a wrongly directed devotion to Mary and at the same time commended, in the highest possible way, the true veneration of his mother.[11] "We have the Old and the New Testament and the Hierarchy to guide us . . . This must be sufficient for our salvation."[12] We are, however, bound to reiterate that this does not take away the great blessing of the "charismatic" element in the Church. It would be quite wrong and indeed contrary to the mind of the Church to claim that the hierarchy was the sole vital impulse in the living Church. We must recognize in all honesty that the prophetic element has its own special part to play in the life of the Church, and at the same time we must also realize that it is only to be expected that the hierarchy, which is responsible for the stability and soundness of the Church's life of faith, should from time to time be alarmed by this "incalculable" element and tend to curb rather than encourage it. Clearly, it would be not only incautious but also unpsychological to allow this incalculable, charismatic element which, because it is so difficult to penetrate, is frequently open to so many interpretations, to develop independently and without restraint. The Holy Ghost may, of course, "play" with human caution. This does not, however, mean to say that we should ever "play" the Holy Ghost's game!

If we introduce undogmatic elements into our sermons we may easily misrepresent the spotless image of the *Assumpta* and cause it to become distorted, in the minds of the faithful, into an image

[11] See also the semi-official warning which Mgr. (now Cardinal) Ottaviani, then Assessor to the Holy Office, had published in the *Osservatore Romano* on 4 November 1951.

[12] Dante, *Il Paradiso*, 5, 73–7, quoted in the above-mentioned article by Cardinal Ottaviani.

different from that of the Gospel, and hence contrary to true dogma. This is something which we should always strenuously avoid. We should not attempt to illuminate the true figure of Mary in all its splendour by intensifying our knowledge of definite apparitions, for all their legitimate importance, and passing this on to the faithful. We should rather give our prayerful attention to the ancient treasure of the Gospel and the essential dogma of Mary. Our aim should always be to bring this Gospel and dogmatic image of Mary more and more into the foreground. This will be a gradual process, but we shall be aided in the task by the intimate devotion to Mary which exists within the believing community of the Church. The ultimate result will be that each member of the Christian community, in union with Christ and his mother, will come every day to the fresh discovery that the whole of the Christian life, in its harsher and in its sweeter aspects, in its moments of extreme tension and in its periods of depression, is pure grace.

THE POWER OF OUR MARIAN PRAYER TO CHRIST

Marian Prayer in General

The believer takes real initiatives in prayer. He does not simply carry out blindly or in apparent freedom what has already been established for a long time in rigid regularity. His prayer is really capable of renewing the face of the earth. Prayer is an intimate experience, based on a personal I–Thou relationship, a living communication between two *free beings* approaching each other in love —a personal communication between God and man. Our *fiat* is never a senseless submission to a fixed and immovable fate. When we say "*Thy* will be done," we are referring to the will of *my* God, to whom *I* turn in prayer and who requires a "decision" from the first moment of and as a direct result of my initiative in prayer. It is, of course, difficult for us to visualize the relationship between our temporal, fleeting condition and the dynamic eternity of God's order which does not pass and which we tend to see, in our imaginations, as a motionless block of granite, impregnable to all attacks of the weather. We must, however, not imagine that God has arranged everything, chronologically speaking, before our prayer. Gabriel Marcel has expressed this idea very well. Eternity may be regarded as the *meaning in depth* of our temporal decision or our prayer of petition. In this way, it is possible to see that my prayer is in reality a genuine initiative on the part of a free creature of God, directed towards the divine and all-embracing Being, whom I, at the moment of my prayer, address as "Thou." What is more, it is also possible to see that this Being has not arranged and decided everything before I come into contact with him, but that he does this in an actual eternal now that brings the moment of my prayer to his immediate attention and creatively controls it. The more intimately we are united to him, the bolder and the more efficacious our initiative in prayer will be. This intimate surrender to God has the effect of bringing our will into harmony with God's loving being. As a consequence of this, anything that the Christian who is intimate with God asks will always be granted to him.

If this is the real explanation of the efficacy of every Christian prayer, it must at once be apparent that the same is bound to apply in a unique and incomparable manner to the supplicatory prayer of Mary, Suppliant Omnipotence, and similarly to our prayer as well, when this is joined to the prayer of our heavenly mother. We should, therefore, be less disposed to claim miracles and be more ready to think in terms of the normal meaning of prayer in our lives. If a child asks his father for a toy and the father gives this toy to him, the child sees in the gift, quite simply, his father's *answer* to his request. This does not exclude the fact that the father may have to buy the toy before giving it to his child, so that, from the *technical* point of view, the toy is the result of an act of buying and selling. From the technical point of view too, a cure, for example, of a mother of a family, for whom I have been praying to God through Mary, may well be the result of medical treatment and care. For me, however—and in actual fact—this cure is God's answer to my prayerful supplication, and it can only be understood as the result of my faith and hope in God, who does not need money to pay the doctor's fees but who, as the Creator, embraces in himself the entire causal relationship between "medical attention" and "cure" and subordinates this to my prayerful, personal experience of Christ through Mary. What might possibly have been no more than a *fait divers* of everyday life without my prayer becomes, because of my prayer, a meaningful event in my life in association with God. Indeed, it is also possible to go further, and say that, from the *human* point of view, the cure might never have taken place without my prayer. The power of prayer can thus be seen in its correct perspective. "Remember, O most gracious Virgin Mary, that never was it known that anyone who fled to thy protection, implored thy help and sought thy intercession, was left unaided."

The Prayer of the Rosary

Psychological structure of the prayer.— As a form of Marian prayer, the Rosary has been repeatedly commended by the Church. It was not the result of a single inspiration, nor was it instituted at any time in a definite and complete form. It came gradually into being as the result of a slow process of growth, in the course of which it has been subjected to many adaptations, changes, additions and omissions. Its development has also been considerably influenced by profane factors. The counting and repetition of the same prayer is such a widespread practice in almost all the ancient religions of the world that it is possible to regard this phenomenon as a universal religious fact. It forms an intimate part of our spiritual and physical make-up.

There is in fact no real difference between the psychological form of the prayer of the Rosary and that of the prayer of the Breviary. Both are oral and at the same time interior forms of prayer. The basic difference between the two is this—in the case of the Rosary the exterior, oral prayer is always made in the same formula. Prayer is, first and foremost, always an event which takes place interiorly, in the soul. What happens exteriorly is also prayer, but only insofar as it is an externalization of the prayerful attitude of the soul. It would, however, be quite wrong to assert that the continuous recitation of Hail Marys was *no more than* an external technique, serving merely to keep the body occupied so that it will not disturb the soul in its flight. The external muttering of Hail Marys is indeed prayer, not simply a technique. This does not mean that the technical aspect is entirely lacking in the spontaneous repetition of the same formula of prayer. An element of pure technique is certainly present, but we should be careful not to overemphasize its importance. Spiritual writers have frequently pointed out that the quiet monotony of the constantly repeated Hail Marys of the Rosary has a tranquillizing effect on the mind. This is demonstrably true—it is quite possible to pray oneself to sleep with the Rosary. Indeed, some people have found the Rosary a very successful and at the same time pious method of inducing sleep and frequently use it for this purpose in bed at night. As the result of various inquiries, it has been established that the muttered, external prayer of the Rosary certainly encourages internal prayer when this is quietly contemplative, unrestrained, emotional and affective, but that it is often an obstacle to concentrated, meditative prayer.

The Rosary, then, is a relatively free form of prayer. Sometimes we concentrate our attention on the Hail Mary itself, and its content. Then, perhaps in the same decade, we let our mind dwell on the mystery of that decade. If our attention should wander away from the mystery the regularity of the constantly repeated formula will spontaneously draw our mind back to the content of the prayer itself. Prayer is a living experience, a life of faith, hope and charity, to which we must do justice even when we are feeling tired, dull or languid. There is, then, an idealistic conception of the Rosary, which may form the real climax of a concentrated life of prayer and which really is such a climax for many people. On the other hand, there is also a realistic interpretation of this form of prayer, and it is this aspect of the Rosary which I propose to discuss further. Anyone who, in the course of pastoral duties, has any contact with the spiritual life of young people is bound to discover sooner or later that the repetition of the Hail Marys, which forms the basis of the prayer of the Rosary, often makes it impossible for many people to concentrate deeply on the mysteries of the Rosary. We must also openly recognize the fact that the Rosary appeals far less to contemporary man than it did to previous generations of Christians. Many people feel too relaxed when they pray the Rosary—they are not spiritually awake, there is too little tension. In comparison with other forms of prayer, which provide moments of intense and profound experience, the Rosary seems diffuse, vague and indecisive. We should not, however, conclude from these sober facts that the Rosary has failed. On the contrary, the Rosary is a most commendable form of prayer. It is particularly suitable, if not for those moments of intense inner experience which we have already mentioned, then certainly for those occasions when the spirit is weary, dull and listless.

Many Christians, anxious to pray often and at the same time well, have come to the conclusion that the Rosary is a godsend. If, then, the Rosary could also be an instrument enabling the soul to make authentic mystical flights, then, at the highest point of such spiritual experiences, the beads will slip from the fingers and the prayer will, *as it were*, become purely interior. In this case the Rosary will have served its purpose. In most cases, however, the Rosary will always remain a prop to prayer in times of spiritual aridity, as investigation has in fact established. As in the case of all forms of prayer, it is the Christian's inward surrender, in childlike faith and love, and his intention in prayer which ultimately determine the essential value of the prayer of the Rosary—his presence before God. The Rosary will animate and constantly renew the Christian's awareness of being in God's presence, even when his spirit is dull and arid and his thoughts are distracted. And, since we all find ourselves in this sort of situation again and again in the course of our mortal lives, the Rosary will always be a salutary form of prayer in the Christian's life of prayer.

A non-Catholic writer once observed that man lives, psychologically speaking, on three levels—at the highest level there is a light zone, at the lowest a dark zone, and between these two there is, merging into the others, a zone of half-light. Let us apply this concept of human psychological experience to the practice of the Rosary. In the dark zone there are many acquired visions, impressions, truths and so on. All these preconscious elements can be *evoked* by our affective attitude of the moment and by ideas which become momentarily clearer in our minds. It is an established psychological fact that mechanical means possess considerable power to evoke dormant truths. The Rosary, in its mechanical aspect, acts in this way, and the repetition of Hail Marys can evoke acquired, but dormant Christian truths in our minds. It enables the latent spiritual treasure of the mind to come quietly to the surface. It is a protracted act of love, involving only a very slight interior activation, a loving "relationship," so to speak, during which one particular and more clearly defined content—for example, the mystery of the Annunciation, or the birth or the death of Christ—will from time to time hover in the foreground of the mind, while our attention is fixed, more or less without any tension being involved, by the beads which we move rhythmically through our fingers.

It will, then, be apparent from the foregoing that no titanic efforts are required to pray the Rosary *in forma*, that is to say, we do not need to exert ourselves to experience the prayer of the Rosary *fully*, both by the exterior recitation of the Hail Marys and by the interior contemplation of the mysteries. We do not need to attempt the impossible and frustrating task of, so to speak, trying to play two pianos at the same time! This would demand too much of us as human beings and would, at the same time, be detrimental to the prayer as an act of love and surrender. When we use the Rosary we should rather allow God to move us and to penetrate the whole of our being. The essence of every act of prayer is to make our will conform to God's will. In the case of the Rosary this is accomplished by a murmuring, almost silent blending of wills. On those frequent occasions when our spirit is lacking in tension, but we still try to pray and instinctively resort to the Rosary, our "Thy will be done" will become a peaceful, and sometimes even indistinct gazing into an atmosphere in which this harmony of wills has, so to speak, *already taken place*, but at the moment of our prayer *finds an echo* in our religious consciousness.

For this reason, the Rosary seems to me to be not so much the reverse of an activating factor in our spiritual life as a reverberation of the life of prayer, in a mind which is quiet, peaceful and perhaps even fatigued. The mind must already have been actively nourished from other sources. These active sources of spiritual nourishment may, for example, be the sacraments of the Eucharist or of penance, private meditation or the public recitation of the Divine Office. It is only if we present the Rosary to young people of today in this light that we shall be able to emphasize its lasting value.

The dogmatic aspect.— The value of the prayer of the Rosary is to be found in its concentration on the saving mystery of the Redemption. It was Christ who brought this redemption, but Mary is actively present in and associated with the whole of this historical order of salvation. The Rosary is a synthetic Christological creed, a *symbolum* or compendium of dogma and doctrine, in the form of a prayer of meditation, a summary, in prayer, of the whole of the dogma of the Redemption.[13] Because its use has become so widespread, the Rosary is clearly a most important weapon in the instruction of the Church community in Christian dogma. The dogmatic faith of the believing community can be confirmed *through prayer*. In prayer we are able to go back into the past and put ourselves in Mary's position. The Rosary enables us to follow her development, the growth of her life. In faith and hope we are able to experience all the phases of the mystery of Christ, to proceed from the joys of the mother and her Child, to go beyond the sufferings endured by the Redeemer and his mother and eventually to reach

---

[13] In the course of the history of the Rosary as a form of prayer, the fifteen mysteries have been variously distributed. Several different variations are still in use in various countries. From the dogmatic point of view, there is need of a thorough revision of the distribution of the mysteries.

the point where we share in Mary's happiness in her Son's victory and triumph. Christ—personal redemption, Redemption itself—is at the centre of this Marian prayer. When we pray the Rosary we are focusing our attention inwardly on the living mysteries of Christ. Outwardly, we do no more than murmur, almost breathlessly, the Hail Marys, while our gaze is directed upwards, in faith, to each mystery in turn. What we are in fact saying to Mary, throughout this inward prayer, is no more than, "Thank you." The prayer of the Rosary can teach us how to model our *fiat* on Mary's "typical" example, and how to express this personal assent to all the various stages of our own lives—in joy, in suffering and in triumph. We shall learn not to allow ourselves to be inspired by the momentary, the transitory circumstances of our life on earth, but to draw our inspiration from the essential, eternal and actual reality of the Redemption, by means of an emptying of ourselves (*exinanitio*) and an elevation of ourselves through God (*exaltatio*). In other words, we shall let the divine Redeemer's human acts of salvation, the saving mysteries to which Mary fully committed herself *as a mother,* inspire us.

God himself entered the world of man and, in his humanity, not only shared in man's fundamental situation but also provided it with its ultimate phase, thereby giving it an entirely new interpretation, so that there was not only human life and death but also resurrection. This basic theme of man's condition can be seen in a Christian perspective in the prayer of the Rosary. It is stripped of that element of human superficiality and human disappointment and frustration with which it is continuously threatened. The Rosary can make us powerfully aware that the *vita ex morte*, the life which surges up out of death and sacrifice, is a religious and moral task occupying the whole of our lives. While praying the Rosary we are also asking Jesus and his mother for the strength to be able to realize this task in our lives.

When we pray the Rosary, we are doing what Mary herself did: "His mother kept all these words in her heart." (Luke 2. 51.) It was by prayerful reflection that she learned how to understand the mystery of Christ and to become fully aware of her own particular place in the economy of the Redemption. It is only by becoming more and more familiar with the "mystery of Christ," which *embraces* the mystery of Mary, that we too shall come to an understanding of our place and our concrete vocation in the redeemed world.

Whenever we ask God for a particular favour through the Rosary we are in fact praying "through Christ our Lord," and this supplication is indissolubly connected with our prayer "through the Queen of the World." We are appealing to the mystery of Christ, which is at the same time intimately associated with the mystery of Mary and, in the concrete sense, *is a Marian mystery*. For the secret of this mother, Mary, is this—her maternal self-identification with the sanctifying activity of her Son. As Christ's mother, she has foreknowledge of his heart and is able to take initiatives to which he gives his *a priori* consent. In the last resort we can understand these initiatives only if we see them as the result of an impulse emanating from Jesus' human heart and directed towards Mary's.

The family Rosary.—Said at home, by all the members of the family, the Rosary is capable of becoming, together with more modern forms of family prayer, a real family "liturgy" with a pure dogmatic orientation. It would be wrong to condemn the family Rosary out of hand as a routine, uninspired performance, sometimes accompanied by such external family activities as darning socks or making clothes for the children. What the Rosary in fact does is to lead the whole family, in prayer and quiet activity, to the foot of God's throne in the proximity of Christ and his mother. The family Rosary is the "Lord, behold thy family, dedicated to thee," the "Thou hast redeemed us," uttered by the Christian family in prayer to its God. During the Rosary the family is exposed to God. When the family assembles to recite the Rosary together this is a time of especial privilege. It is then that the family, as a community, experiences God as its unifying factor. The family ties of love become firmer and the members are more conscious of these ties as characteristic of the family as such and differentiated from the all-embracing ties of Christian *caritas*. The family Rosary enables the family to become a saving community in microcosm, in which the temporal, and sometimes so pre-occupying needs of the family fall into their proper place within the greater context of the one vital necessity—that God's *kingdom* may *come*, that his will be done *on earth*, here in *this family*, as it is in heaven.

The Rosary is for the family what Compline is for the religious community—"Keep us, O Lord, as the apple of thine eye." While the prayer pursues its steady, rhythmic course, the many family problems which beset him are passing fleetingly through the father's tired mind and the mother is thinking of the baby she is carrying or of the children around her, each with its own particular difficulty. All this can be seen, throughout the quiet progress of the Rosary, in the light of the redeeming mystery of Christ and, in peaceful simplicity, the family learns to entrust everything to the mother of the miracle of Cana and of the whole redemption of mankind. In the words of the Flemish poet, Guido Gezelle, "How many times have I found, whenever I have come to appeal to thee, that thou hast healed the aching wounds of my heart!"

5

CONCLUSION: OUR LIFE,
OUR SWEETNESS AND OUR HOPE

IT WILL, OF COURSE, be apparent, from the entire contents of this book, that Mary is a divine mystery whose ultimate depths we shall never be able to fathom so long as we are in this world. It is clear that she must be a creature of matchless wonder, this *Immaculata* and *Assumpta*, with whom even the most physically and spiritually beautiful woman in the world cannot in any way be compared— *Nec primam similem visa est nec habere sequentem*! What the power of her supplication means in terms of religious reality for all of us is a mystery which is totally inseparable from the mystery of Christ. What is more, the power of her supplication on *your* behalf will always be beyond *my* comprehension, and it will never be possible for *you* to grasp what this power means for *me*. For we are dealing here with a region of experience which lies outside the scope of human discussion—the most intimate of all relationships, that of the little child and its mother.

Mary is not only the mother of those who have reached a high level of mystical experience in their lives. She is also, in a certain sense, the *special* mother of those who are still caught up in the habits of sin. It was by God's exceptional mercy that she remained unacquainted with sin, and without this mercy she would never have been immaculate. For this reason, she shows her gratitude to God by taking on the function of "Refuge of Sinners." Bernanos describes this function beautifully in his book, *Journal d'un curé de campagne*: "For she was *born* without sin—in what amazing isolation! . . . This poor human race of ours is not worth very much, but

172

childhood always moves her heart to deep compassion. The ignorance of little children makes her lower her eyes—those eyes which know good and evil, those eyes which have seen so many things! But, after all, it isn't simply a question of ignorance alone. The Virgin was Innocence. . . . The eyes of our Lady are the only real child-eyes that have ever been raised to our shame and sorrow. Yes . . . to pray to her as you should you must feel those eyes of hers upon you: they are not indulgent—for there is no indulgence without something of bitter experience—they are eyes of gentle pity, wondering sadness, and with something more in them, never known or expressed, something which makes her *younger than sin*. . . ."[1] The sinner who looks up to Mary for help can hope to be liberated from his sinful situation. She is our advocate, the one to whom we appeal for help in every difficult situation. She is our life, our sweetness and our hope.

During her life on this earth Mary surrendered unconditionally to the living God whenever she found herself in difficulty. This should always be an encouragement to us. We are all too readily inclined to believe, simply because we are Christians, go to church on Sundays and fulfil our Christian duties, that everything in our lives is bound to be plain sailing—that we should, as a matter of course, never encounter any real adversity, especially in our family lives. We forget so easily that religion is in no sense a life-insurance policy against the misfortunes of this world. But religion is effective,

[1] *The Diary of a Country Priest,* trans. Pamela Morris (New York, Macmillan). "Car enfin, elle était née sans péché, quelle solitude étonnante! . . . Certes, notre pauvre espèce ne vaut pas cher, mais l'enfance émeut toujours ses entrailles, l'ignorance des petits lui fait baisser les yeux—ses yeux qui savent le bien et le mal, ses yeux qui ont vu tant de choses! Mais ce n'est que l'ignorance après tout. La Vierge était l'Innocence . . . Le regard de la Vierge est le seul regard vraiment enfantin, le seul vrai regard d'enfant qui se soit jamais levé sur notre honte et notre malheur. Oui . . . pour la bien prier, il faut sentir sur soi ce regard qui n'est pas tout à fait celui de l'indulgence—car l'indulgence ne va pas sans quelque expérience amère— mais la tendre compassion, de la surprise douloureuse, d'on ne sait quel sentiment encore, inconcevable, inexprimable, qui la fait *plus jeune que le péché.*" (Paris, Librairie Plon [1936], pp. 231 f.) (Part of the text quoted by the author does not appear in the English edition. [Tr.].)

of course, in that essential part of our human existence which can never be satisfied by worldly possessions or annihilated by any of the adversities which we are likely to meet in this life. Religion is concerned with our longing for the living God and with our need for all that can only come from the quality of motherhood. The essence of our religious life is sacrificial love.

Mary became the mother of this sacrificial love by carrying God himself in her arms as her own Child. That is why the statue of Mary and the Holy Child in the house can be such a sound support to the family in times of trouble. Above all, Mary knows what it is to suffer as a human being. She endured human suffering during the Flight into Egypt. She experienced it again when the twelve-year-old Jesus was lost for three days. Later, when her Son put a distance between himself and her with the beginning of his public life, she once again suffered acutely. A grown-up son is still his mother's boy —however mature he may be, he never ceases, as far as she is concerned, to be "a child." How can we, then, imagine Mary's human agony when her Child met her on the way to Calvary and later, when she saw him, her divine Child, die on the Cross? And what human suffering did she not experience when finally she took the dead Jesus on her lap and clasped his body to her breast—she whose womb had been the witness of a mystery which heralded the salvation and redemption of the world?

Our devotion to Mary, then, must go right to the heart of the living Christian faith. It must be a *fiat* which goes, in sacrificial love, to the ultimate limit. Life is only good if it is offered as a gift. Life is love, a love which gives. The gift which we make of our love, our life, must be made in a spirit of pure self-forgetfulness. If we do this, our suffering will become a relic of Christ's redeeming death, a priceless relic which will find its resting-place, like the crucified Christ's, in the arms of Mary, his and our mother. She will take the racked treasure of our suffering on her knees and place it beside the tortured relic of Christ's body. Her lap contains all the suffering of the whole of humanity, the countless, ever-growing number of wounds of a human race which is continuously crucified. She is the great *Pietà* who casts her mother's cloak of mercy over our suffering humanity. She is the living womb in which, as in a second act of bodily motherhood, we are carried for the nine long months of our lives until we at last come to the glory of redemption and resurrection.

Mary is the loving heart in our lives. She is objective and even matter-of-fact, but, because she has herself experienced and shared them, she always understands our difficulties in life and has sympathy for us. With unfailing solicitude she finds out what our needs are and, with the straightforward simplicity of a mother, she brings them to the attention of God who, in Jesus, was and still is her Child, her "Boy"—"They have no wine!" If only we could spend but one single moment listening to Mary's wordless conversation about us with Jesus! If we could but catch a single glimpse of her face when she looks at her Son with a glance which tells him, "They have no wine," "They have no money," "They are in terrible distress," "Their father is ill and their mother has eight children already," "They want so much to express their love for each other physically, but their circumstances make it so difficult for them to have another child," "Their mother has run away from home— their father has told them that she has gone on a long journey and he does not know when she will come back. . . ."

Let us, however, always take care never to forget one thing. This conversation in heaven between Mary, our glorified mother, and Christ, her glorified Son, will only bring a blessing into our lives on condition that we are ever mindful of the words that Mary addressed to the waiters at the marriage feast in Cana: "Whatsoever he [my Son] shall say to you, do ye." (John 2. 5.) Then, and then only, may you taste what she will give you through her divine Son, and then you will have to acknowledge, like the guests at the marriage feast, "They have kept the good wine until now."

> Parce que vous êtes là pour toujours, simplement
>   parce que vous êtes Marie,
> simplement parce que vous existez, Mère de Jésus-Christ,
>   soyez remerciée.[2]

[2] Paul Claudel, *Poèmes de guerre*, "La Vierge à midi."